Break Free From Overthinking : 10 Effektive Strategies For Stress Relief And Mental Clarity

Benjamin Drath

Published by Benjamin Drath, 2023.

While every precaution has been taken in the preparation of this book, the publisher assumes no responsibility for errors or omissions, or for damages resulting from the use of the information contained herein.

BREAK FREE FROM OVERTHINKING : 10 EFFEKTIVE STRATEGIES FOR STRESS RELIEF AND MENTAL CLARITY

First edition. July 21, 2023.

ISBN: 979-8223756378

Written by Benjamin Drath.

Table of Contents

Welcome to "Break free from overthinking: 40 Strategies for stress relief and mental clarity." In a world filled with constant distractions, pressures, and endless streams of information, it's easy to find ourselves trapped in the cycle of overthinking. Our minds become overwhelmed with thoughts, worries, and self-doubt, hindering our ability to find peace, make decisions, and live in the present moment.

But fear not, for within the pages of this book, you will discover a comprehensive guide to breaking free from the overthinking trap. Through 40 powerful strategies, we will explore various techniques, practices, and mindset shifts that will empower you to relieve stress, cultivate mental clarity, and embrace a more balanced and fulfilling life.

Overthinking not only takes a toll on our mental health but also affects our overall well-being, relationships, and productivity. It drains our energy, hampers our decision-making abilities, and robs us of the joy of the present moment. However, with the right tools and a commitment to self-growth, you can reclaim control over your thoughts and emotions, and experience the freedom and peace that come with a clear and calm mind.

Each chapter in this book is designed to provide you with practical strategies and insights that you can apply in your daily life. From understanding the overthinking trap and its impact on mental health to harnessing the power of mindfulness, cultivating self-awareness, and developing a growth mindset, you will embark on a transformative journey of self-discovery.

You will learn how to let go of negative thought patterns, embrace imperfection, and release regrets. Journaling techniques, gratitude practices, and the importance of creating a supportive environment will be explored to help you gain clarity and emotional release. You will also discover the significance of nurturing healthy relationships, setting boundaries, and managing your time effectively to reduce overthinking.

Throughout this book, you will be introduced to various mindfulness techniques, such as visualization, creativity, and breathwork, which can enhance mental clarity and provide a sense of calm. Additionally, strategies for handling uncertainty, improving sleep and rest, and redirecting overthinking energy into productivity will be shared.

Embracing the power of self-care, practicing forgiveness, and developing emotional intelligence will further support your journey towards breaking free from overthinking. You will also explore the role of technology, decision-making, and intuition in promoting mental clarity and overall well-being.

As you progress through the chapters, you will be encouraged to engage in reflective exercises, take actionable steps, and integrate these strategies into your daily life. With perseverance and commitment, you will witness the transformation of your mindset, gain a deeper understanding of yourself, and experience a newfound sense of freedom and clarity.

So, are you ready to embark on this transformative journey? Are you ready to release the chains of overthinking and embrace a life filled with mental clarity, peace, and fulfillment? If your answer is a resounding yes, then let us begin. Together, we will navigate the path to lasting freedom from overthinking, one chapter at a time.

Chapter 1: Understanding the overthinking trap.

———

Introduction:

In today's fast-paced and complex world, the human mind often becomes entangled in the web of overthinking. This chapter aims to provide a comprehensive understanding of the overthinking trap, its impact on our lives, and how it affects our mental well-being. By unraveling the intricacies of overthinking, we can begin to find effective strategies to break free and regain control of our thoughts and emotions.

Defining overthinking:

Overthinking can be described as a process where individuals excessively dwell on their thoughts, worries, or concerns. It involves repetitive rumination, analyzing situations from various angles, and often leads to an overwhelming and unproductive mental state. Overthinking tends to be fueled by fear, anxiety, perfectionism, and a need for control.

The downside of overthinking:

While thinking is a natural and necessary cognitive process, overthinking can have detrimental effects on our mental health and overall well-being. The constant barrage of negative thoughts and self-doubt can contribute to increased stress levels, anxiety disorders, and even depression. Overthinking hinders decision-making, impairs problem-solving abilities, and steals away our present moment awareness.

Understanding the causes:

Various factors contribute to the development of the overthinking trap. Past experiences, traumas, and conditioning can influence our thinking patterns. Unrealistic expectations, fear of failure, and a desire for perfection can further exacerbate overthinking tendencies. Social pressures, comparisons, and information overload in the digital age also play a significant role in perpetuating the cycle of overthinking.

The vicious cycle of overthinking:

Overthinking often follows a cyclic pattern. It begins with a triggering event or thought that leads to excessive analysis and rumination. This constant mental churn perpetuates the cycle, trapping individuals in a loop of negative thoughts and emotions. The more we overthink, the more overwhelmed and disconnected we feel from the present moment.

Impact on mental well-being:

Overthinking takes a toll on our mental well-being in various ways. It increases stress levels, disrupts sleep patterns, and drains our energy. Chronic overthinking can lead to a heightened state of anxiety, leaving individuals feeling trapped, unable to escape the incessant mental chatter. It also affects our relationships, as overthinkers often struggle with communication, intimacy, and emotional vulnerability.

Recognizing overthinking patterns:

To break free from the overthinking trap, it is crucial to recognize the patterns and triggers that fuel our overthinking tendencies. By developing self-awareness, we can identify the thoughts, situations, or emotions that initiate the cycle of overthinking. This awareness empowers us to intervene and redirect our focus towards more productive and positive thinking patterns.

Embracing mindfulness:

One effective approach to understanding and overcoming overthinking is through the practice of mindfulness. Mindfulness cultivates present moment awareness and non-judgmental observation of our thoughts and emotions. By learning to observe our thoughts without attachment or judgment, we can detach ourselves from the overthinking process and find clarity and peace in the present moment.

Conclusion:

Understanding the overthinking trap is the first step towards breaking free from its grasp. By recognizing the causes, patterns, and impacts of overthinking, we gain the necessary tools to regain control over our thoughts and emotions. In the upcoming chapters, we will explore effective strategies and techniques that can help relieve stress, foster mental clarity, and guide us towards a more balanced and mindful way of living. Remember, you have the power to break free from the overthinking trap and embrace a more peaceful and present existence.

Chapter 2: The impact of overthinking on mental health.

───

I ntroduction:

In this chapter, we delve into the profound impact that overthinking can have on our mental health. Overthinking is not merely a harmless habit but a persistent state of mind that can significantly affect our overall well-being. By understanding how overthinking affects our mental health, we can take proactive steps to address and mitigate its negative consequences.

The connection between overthinking and mental health:

Overthinking is closely linked to mental health issues such as anxiety and depression. The constant rumination and excessive worry associated with overthinking can create a vicious cycle that exacerbates these conditions. The repetitive nature of overthinking prevents individuals from finding relief and achieving mental clarity, leading to a deterioration in their emotional and psychological well-being.

Increased levels of stress:

Overthinking places an immense burden on our minds, leading to heightened levels of stress. As our thoughts spiral out of control, our bodies respond by releasing stress hormones, such as cortisol. Prolonged exposure to these hormones can have detrimental effects on our physical and mental health, including increased blood pressure, weakened immune system, and impaired cognitive function.

Anxiety disorders:

Overthinking is a breeding ground for anxiety disorders. When we excessively focus on negative thoughts and worst-case scenarios, we fuel our anxiety, leading to a constant state of apprehension and worry. Generalized anxiety disorder (GAD), panic disorder, and social anxiety disorder are common conditions that can arise from chronic overthinking.

Impact on decision-making:

Overthinking hinders effective decision-making. When caught in the overthinking trap, we become trapped in a cycle of analysis paralysis, struggling to make choices due to excessive rumination and fear of making the wrong decision. This not only increases stress but also hampers our ability to move forward and achieve our goals.

Relationship strain:

Overthinking can strain relationships. Constantly analyzing interactions, questioning intentions, and overinterpreting signals can lead to misunderstandings and conflicts. Overthinkers may find it challenging to trust others, express their needs, or engage in open and honest communication, which can negatively impact their relationships and overall social well-being.

Disrupted sleep patterns:

The overactive mind of an overthinker often disrupts sleep patterns. Intrusive thoughts, worries, and anxiety can make it difficult to fall asleep and stay asleep, leading to sleep deprivation and its associated consequences. Lack of quality sleep further exacerbates mental health issues, impairs cognitive function, and weakens our overall well-being.

Negative self-talk and self-esteem:

Overthinking is often accompanied by negative self-talk and self-criticism. The constant barrage of self-doubt, self-judgment, and self-sabotaging thoughts erodes our self-esteem and self-worth. Overthinkers may develop a distorted perception of themselves, believing they are incapable, unworthy, or constantly making mistakes.

Breaking free for better mental health:

Recognizing the detrimental impact of overthinking on our mental health is the first step towards breaking free from its grip. It is crucial to develop strategies that promote self-compassion, challenge negative thoughts, and cultivate a positive mindset. Seeking professional help, such as therapy or counseling, can provide valuable support and guidance in managing overthinking and its effects on mental health.

Conclusion:

The impact of overthinking on mental health is undeniable. It affects our stress levels, fuels anxiety disorders, impairs decision-making, strains relationships, disrupts sleep patterns, and damages self-esteem. Understanding the intricate connection between overthinking and mental health empowers us to take proactive steps to address and overcome this harmful habit. In the following chapters, we will explore effective strategies to relieve stress, declutter the mind, and regain mental clarity, ultimately fostering improved mental well-being. Remember, you have the power to break free from the grip of overthinking and cultivate a healthier state of mind.

One of the key steps in mitigating the impact of overthinking on mental health is to develop self-awareness. By observing our thought patterns and recognizing when we are caught in the cycle of overthinking, we can begin to interrupt and redirect our thoughts. Mindfulness practices, such as meditation and deep breathing exercises, can be instrumental in increasing self-awareness and bringing our attention back to the present moment.

In addition to self-awareness, it is essential to challenge the validity of our thoughts. Overthinkers often engage in cognitive distortions, where they catastrophize or engage in all-or-nothing thinking. By questioning the accuracy and rationality of these thoughts, we can reframe them in a more realistic and balanced manner. This process involves examining evidence, considering alternative perspectives, and focusing on solutions rather than dwelling on problems.

Cultivating self-compassion is another vital aspect of addressing the impact of overthinking on mental health. Overthinkers tend to be excessively self-critical, placing unrealistic expectations on themselves and berating themselves for perceived failures. Practicing self-compassion involves treating ourselves with kindness, understanding, and acceptance. It entails acknowledging that making mistakes and experiencing challenges are part of being human and extending the same compassion to ourselves that we would to a friend in need.

Building a strong support system is also crucial for maintaining good mental health while combating overthinking. Sharing our concerns and feelings with trusted friends, family members, or mental health professionals can provide much-needed perspective, validation, and guidance. Connecting with others who have experienced similar challenges can also be beneficial, as it fosters a sense of belonging and reminds us that we are not alone in our struggles.

Engaging in activities that promote relaxation and stress reduction is essential for managing the impact of overthinking on mental health. Engaging in regular exercise, practicing hobbies, spending time in nature, and incorporating relaxation techniques like yoga or tai chi can help to alleviate stress, calm the mind, and promote overall well-being.

In some cases, professional intervention may be necessary to address the severe impact of overthinking on mental health. Cognitive-behavioral therapy (CBT) is a widely recognized and effective approach for treating overthinking and related mental health conditions. A trained therapist can guide individuals in identifying and modifying maladaptive thinking patterns, providing practical tools and strategies to manage overthinking and its consequences.

In conclusion, the impact of overthinking on mental health is significant, affecting various aspects of our well-being. Recognizing the connection between overthinking and mental health allows us to take proactive steps to address and mitigate its negative effects. Through self-awareness, challenging distorted thoughts, cultivating self-compassion, building a support system, engaging in relaxation activities, and seeking professional help when needed, we can break free from the overthinking trap and promote better mental health. Remember, you have the power to reclaim control over your thoughts and live a more balanced and fulfilling life.

Chapter 3: Cultivating self-awareness to combat overthinking.

Introduction:

In this chapter, we explore the importance of self-awareness as a powerful tool in combating overthinking. By developing a deep understanding of our thoughts, emotions, and behavioral patterns, we can gain insight into the root causes of overthinking and take proactive steps to break free from its grasp. Cultivating self-awareness is the key to reclaiming control over our minds and fostering mental clarity.

The essence of self-awareness:

Self-awareness is the ability to observe and understand our thoughts, feelings, and actions without judgment or attachment. It involves becoming conscious of the present moment and being attuned to our internal experiences. By practicing self-awareness, we can recognize when we are caught in the cycle of overthinking and take intentional steps to redirect our focus.

Identifying overthinking patterns:

Through self-awareness, we can identify the patterns and triggers that contribute to our overthinking tendencies. By paying attention to our thoughts and emotions, we become aware of recurring themes, excessive rumination, and the situations that provoke overthinking. This awareness empowers us to intervene and choose alternative, more constructive thought patterns.

Practicing mindful observation:

Mindful observation is a fundamental aspect of self-awareness. By observing our thoughts, emotions, and bodily sensations without judgment, we develop a deeper understanding of our internal landscape. Mindfulness practices such as meditation, body scans, and mindful breathing can help cultivate this skill.

Through mindful observation, we can detach ourselves from the constant stream of thoughts and create space for clarity and insight.

Emotional awareness:

Emotional awareness is an integral part of self-awareness. By tuning into our emotions, we can uncover the underlying causes of overthinking. Emotions serve as valuable indicators of our internal state, highlighting areas of stress, anxiety, or unresolved issues. By acknowledging and processing these emotions, we can address their root causes and prevent them from fueling overthinking.

Recognizing cognitive distortions:

Self-awareness enables us to identify and challenge cognitive distortions—habitual thought patterns that contribute to overthinking. Common distortions include black-and-white thinking, catastrophizing, mind-reading, and negative self-talk. By recognizing these distortions, we can actively replace them with more balanced and realistic thoughts, fostering a healthier mindset and reducing overthinking tendencies.

Journaling for self-reflection:

Journaling is a powerful tool for cultivating self-awareness. By expressing our thoughts and feelings on paper, we gain clarity and insight into our overthinking patterns. Regular journaling allows us to track our progress, identify recurring themes, and explore alternative perspectives. It serves as a safe and private space to explore our inner world and gain a deeper understanding of ourselves.

Seeking feedback and perspective:

Another way to enhance self-awareness is by seeking feedback from trusted individuals. Trusted friends, family members, or mentors can offer valuable insights into our blind spots and provide a fresh perspective on our overthinking tendencies. Their observations and feedback can help us gain a more comprehensive understanding of our patterns and behaviors.

Practicing self-reflection:

Self-reflection is a deliberate practice of introspection and self-examination. By setting aside dedicated time for self-reflection, we create opportunities to explore our thoughts, emotions, and behaviors. Asking ourselves probing questions, such as "What triggers my overthinking?" or "How does overthinking impact my life?" allows us to delve deeper into our patterns and make meaningful connections.

Building a supportive mindset:

Self-awareness enables us to cultivate a supportive mindset toward ourselves. Instead of berating ourselves for overthinking, we can practice self-compassion and self-acceptance. Embracing imperfections and treating ourselves with kindness fosters a nurturing environment for growth and change within our own minds. By developing a supportive mindset, we shift our focus from self-criticism to self-care, allowing ourselves space to learn and evolve.

Embracing vulnerability and authenticity:

Self-awareness also involves embracing vulnerability and authenticity. It requires us to acknowledge and accept our strengths, weaknesses, and limitations without judgment. When we allow ourselves to be authentic and vulnerable, we create opportunities for growth, connection, and self-acceptance. Embracing our true selves allows us to navigate life with more clarity and confidence, reducing the need for overthinking.

Cultivating present moment awareness:

A crucial aspect of self-awareness is cultivating present moment awareness. Overthinking often pulls us into the past or propels us into the future, robbing us of the present moment. By consciously redirecting our attention to the here and now, we can break free from the overthinking trap. Practices such as mindfulness meditation, grounding techniques, and sensory awareness exercises help anchor us in the present moment, fostering mental clarity and peace.

Developing intuition and inner guidance:

Self-awareness also involves honing our intuition and inner guidance. By tuning in to our inner voice, we can access valuable insights and guidance. Intuition serves as a powerful compass, guiding us towards decisions and actions aligned with our authentic selves. By trusting our intuition, we can reduce the need for excessive analysis and overthinking, making choices that resonate with our true desires and values.

Consistency and continual practice:

Cultivating self-awareness is an ongoing journey that requires consistency and continual practice. It is not a destination to reach but a skill to develop and refine over time. Regularly dedicating time to self-reflection, mindfulness practices, journaling, and seeking feedback helps us deepen our self-awareness and strengthen our ability to combat overthinking effectively.

Overcoming resistance and fear:

It is important to acknowledge that developing self-awareness can be challenging at times. We may encounter resistance, fear, or discomfort as we confront our thoughts, emotions, and patterns. However, by gently leaning into these challenges and embracing them as opportunities for growth, we can transcend our limitations and expand our self-awareness.

Conclusion:

Cultivating self-awareness is a transformative process that empowers us to combat overthinking and reclaim control over our minds. Through self-observation, emotional awareness, challenging cognitive distortions, journaling, seeking feedback, self-reflection, and embracing vulnerability, we deepen our understanding of ourselves and our patterns. By developing a supportive mindset, cultivating present moment awareness, and honing our intuition, we can navigate life with clarity, authenticity, and mental freedom. Remember, self-awareness is the key to breaking free from the overthinking trap and living a more conscious, balanced, and fulfilling life.

Chapter 4: Harnessing the power of mindfulness for stress relief.

———

Introduction:

In this chapter, we explore the transformative power of mindfulness as a tool for stress relief. Mindfulness is the practice of intentionally bringing our attention to the present moment without judgment. By cultivating a state of mindfulness, we can alleviate stress, reduce overthinking, and enhance our overall well-being. In this chapter, we will delve into various mindfulness techniques and strategies that can help us navigate stress and find inner calm.

Understanding stress and its impact:

Stress is an inevitable part of life, and its impact on our physical and mental health can be significant. Chronic stress can lead to a wide range of health issues, including anxiety, depression, insomnia, and weakened immune function. Overthinking often amplifies stress, creating a cycle that can be difficult to break. By harnessing the power of mindfulness, we can interrupt this cycle and cultivate a greater sense of calm and resilience.

The basics of mindfulness:

Mindfulness involves deliberately paying attention to the present moment, with an attitude of curiosity and acceptance. It is about fully experiencing and embracing the here and now, rather than getting caught up in regrets about the past or worries about the future. Through mindfulness, we can cultivate a non-judgmental awareness of our thoughts, emotions, and sensations, allowing us to respond to stress in a more skillful manner.

Practicing mindful breathing:

One of the foundational mindfulness practices is mindful breathing. By focusing our attention on the sensation of the breath entering and leaving our body, we anchor ourselves in the present moment. The breath serves as an anchor, bringing us back whenever our thoughts start to wander. Mindful breathing can be practiced anywhere, at any time, providing an instant source of calm and stress relief.

Body scan meditation:

Body scan meditation is a mindfulness practice that involves systematically bringing our attention to different parts of the body, from head to toe. It helps us develop a deeper connection with our physical sensations, promoting relaxation and releasing tension. By mindfully scanning our body, we become aware of areas of stress or discomfort and can intentionally release and relax them, alleviating physical and mental tension.

Mindful walking:

Mindful walking is a form of meditation that involves walking slowly and deliberately, paying attention to the sensations of each step. As we walk, we bring our attention to the movement of our feet, the contact with the ground, and the sensations in our body. Mindful walking not only helps us ground ourselves in the present moment but also allows us to connect with nature and the environment around us, fostering a sense of calm and appreciation.

Mindful eating:

Eating mindfully involves bringing our full attention to the experience of eating, savoring each bite without distractions. By slowing down and paying attention to the flavors, textures, and smells of our food, we cultivate a deeper sense of enjoyment and satisfaction. Mindful eating also helps us develop a healthier relationship with food, as we become more attuned to our body's hunger and fullness cues.

Mindful self-compassion:

Mindfulness can also be extended to self-compassion, which involves treating ourselves with kindness and understanding during times of stress. Instead of engaging in self-criticism or judgment, we practice self-compassion by acknowledging our struggles, offering ourselves support and comfort, and reminding ourselves that we are only human. Cultivating self-compassion allows us to navigate stress with greater resilience and gentleness.

Integrating mindfulness into daily life:

Mindfulness is not just a formal practice; it is a way of life. It can be integrated into our daily activities, such as washing dishes, brushing our teeth, or commuting to work. By bringing a mindful presence to these everyday tasks, we can transform them into opportunities for relaxation and stress relief. For example, while washing dishes, we can focus on the sensations of the warm water, the texture of the dishes, and the gentle movements of our hands. By engaging our senses and fully immersing ourselves in the present moment, we can turn mundane activities into mindful experiences that bring us a sense of calm and groundedness.

Bringing mindfulness to stressful situations:

Mindfulness can also be particularly helpful during challenging and stressful situations. When faced with a stressful event or a difficult conversation, we can pause and take a few deep breaths to center ourselves. By consciously bringing our attention to the present moment, we can respond with greater clarity and composure, rather than reacting impulsively based on our automatic patterns of thinking.

The benefits of regular mindfulness practice:

Engaging in regular mindfulness practice offers a wide range of benefits for stress relief and overall well-being. Research has shown that mindfulness reduces levels of the stress hormone cortisol, lowers blood pressure, and improves immune function. It also enhances our ability to regulate emotions, cultivates a sense of inner peace, and improves our overall mental clarity and focus. By incorporating mindfulness into our daily routine, we can proactively manage stress and build resilience.

Overcoming common challenges in mindfulness practice:

While mindfulness offers numerous benefits, it is important to acknowledge that it can be challenging at times. Our minds may wander, and we may encounter resistance or impatience. However, these challenges are part of the practice itself. When we notice our minds drifting or becoming restless, we gently bring our attention back to the present moment without judgment. Gradually, with consistent practice, we develop greater focus and resilience.

Cultivating a mindful lifestyle:

Beyond formal mindfulness practices, cultivating a mindful lifestyle involves adopting certain attitudes and perspectives. It involves cultivating gratitude, being fully present in our interactions with others, and engaging in activities that nourish our mind, body, and spirit. It also means setting healthy boundaries, managing our time wisely, and prioritizing self-care. By embracing a mindful lifestyle, we create a supportive foundation for stress relief and overall well-being.

Conclusion:

In this chapter, we explored the power of mindfulness as a tool for stress relief. By practicing mindfulness, we can cultivate a greater sense of present moment awareness, reduce overthinking, and enhance our overall well-being. From mindful breathing and body scan meditations to incorporating mindfulness into daily activities and challenging situations, there are various techniques that can be embraced. By integrating mindfulness into our lives and adopting a mindful lifestyle, we can navigate stress with greater ease, find inner calm, and live with more clarity and balance. Remember, mindfulness is a lifelong practice that can bring profound positive changes to our lives.

Chapter 5: Developing a growth mindset to overcome overthinking.

———

I ntroduction:

In this chapter, we explore the concept of a growth mindset as a powerful tool to overcome overthinking. A growth mindset is the belief that our abilities and intelligence can be developed through dedication, effort, and a willingness to learn. By cultivating a growth mindset, we can shift our perspective on challenges, setbacks, and failures, allowing us to break free from the grip of overthinking and embrace a more positive and proactive approach to life.

Understanding fixed and growth mindsets:

The mindset we adopt significantly influences how we perceive ourselves, our abilities, and our potential for growth. A fixed mindset is characterized by the belief that our abilities are fixed traits, and we have a limited capacity for improvement. This mindset often leads to self-doubt, fear of failure, and a tendency to overthink. On the other hand, a growth mindset recognizes that intelligence, talents, and skills can be developed through effort, practice, and learning. By embracing a growth mindset, we open ourselves up to new possibilities and break free from the limitations of overthinking.

Embracing challenges as opportunities:

One of the fundamental aspects of a growth mindset is embracing challenges as opportunities for growth and learning. Instead of shying away from difficult tasks or avoiding potential failure, individuals with a growth mindset view challenges as stepping stones toward improvement. By reframing challenges as opportunities to expand our abilities and knowledge, we can overcome the fear of failure and engage in a more proactive and resilient approach to life.

Cultivating a positive relationship with failure:

Failure is an inevitable part of life, and how we perceive and respond to failure greatly influences our mindset. Individuals with a growth mindset view failure as a valuable learning experience rather than a reflection of their worth or abilities. They understand that setbacks and mistakes provide valuable feedback and insights that can guide future growth and improvement. By embracing failure as a natural part of the learning process, we can release the fear of making mistakes and reduce overthinking.

Developing a love for learning:

A growth mindset nurtures a love for learning and a curiosity about the world. Individuals with a growth mindset see learning as a lifelong journey rather than a destination. They actively seek out new knowledge, skills, and experiences, and they understand that growth and development require continuous learning and improvement. By cultivating a love for learning, we can shift our focus from overthinking and self-doubt to the joy of exploration and personal growth.

Embracing effort and persistence:

In a growth mindset, effort and persistence are celebrated and valued. Individuals with this mindset understand that success is not solely based on innate talent but also on the willingness to put in consistent effort and persevere in the face of challenges. By embracing effort and persistence, we develop resilience, determination, and a stronger sense of self-belief, reducing the need for overthinking and self-doubt.

Challenging negative self-talk:

Negative self-talk is a common trap of overthinking. Individuals with a growth mindset actively challenge and replace negative self-talk with more positive and constructive thoughts. They understand that their inner dialogue greatly influences their mindset and actions. By practicing self-awareness and mindfulness, we can catch negative self-talk in its tracks and consciously replace it with affirming and empowering statements that support our growth and development.

Seeking feedback and embracing criticism:

In a growth mindset, feedback and constructive criticism are seen as valuable tools for growth and improvement. Individuals with this mindset actively seek feedback from others, view it as an opportunity to learn and grow, and use it to refine their skills and abilities. By embracing feedback and criticism with an open mind, we can overcome the fear of judgment and utilize the insights gained to propel our personal and professional development.

Celebrating progress and small wins:

In a growth mindset, it is essential to celebrate progress and small wins along the way. Acknowledging and appreciating the steps we take towards our goals reinforces a positive and proactive mindset. By recognizing our achievements, no matter how small they may seem, we build confidence, motivation, and a sense of momentum. Celebrating progress allows us to shift our focus from overthinking and self-criticism to a more optimistic and empowering perspective.

Fostering resilience and adaptability:

A growth mindset cultivates resilience and adaptability in the face of challenges and setbacks. Individuals with this mindset understand that setbacks are temporary and can be overcome with effort, perseverance, and a willingness to adapt. They view obstacles as opportunities for growth and use them as stepping stones to further develop their skills and abilities. By fostering resilience and adaptability, we reduce the impact of overthinking, as we become more adept at navigating and bouncing back from challenges.

Surrounding yourself with supportive networks:

Developing a growth mindset is greatly influenced by the environment we surround ourselves with. It is essential to seek out supportive networks and communities that foster a growth mindset. Surrounding ourselves with individuals who believe in our potential, encourage our growth, and provide constructive feedback can significantly impact our mindset and help us overcome overthinking. Through collaboration, shared learning, and support, we can enhance our growth mindset and continue to thrive.

Practicing gratitude and positivity:

Cultivating a growth mindset involves practicing gratitude and maintaining a positive outlook. By acknowledging and appreciating the good in our lives, we shift our focus from negative thoughts and overthinking to a more optimistic perspective. Gratitude and positivity fuel our motivation, resilience, and overall well-being. By incorporating gratitude practices and positive affirmations into our daily routine, we nurture a growth mindset and reduce the tendency to get caught up in overthinking.

Conclusion:

In this chapter, we explored the power of developing a growth mindset to overcome overthinking. By embracing challenges as opportunities, cultivating a positive relationship with failure, and fostering a love for learning, we can shift our mindset from fixed to growth. Embracing effort, seeking feedback, and celebrating progress are crucial steps in developing a growth mindset. By surrounding ourselves with supportive networks and practicing gratitude and positivity, we can reinforce our growth mindset and overcome the limitations of overthinking. Remember, developing a growth mindset is an ongoing process that requires self-reflection, conscious effort, and a commitment to personal growth.

Chapter 6: The art of letting go: Releasing negative thought patterns.

Introduction:

In this chapter, we delve into the art of letting go and explore strategies for releasing negative thought patterns. Overthinking often stems from dwelling on negative thoughts, worries, and self-doubt. By learning to let go of these patterns, we can free ourselves from their grip and cultivate a more positive and empowered mindset. In this chapter, we will explore various techniques and practices that can help us release negative thought patterns and embrace a more peaceful and balanced state of mind.

Understanding the impact of negative thought patterns:

Negative thought patterns can significantly impact our mental well-being and overall outlook on life. They can lead to increased stress, anxiety, and a distorted perception of reality. Over time, repetitive negative thoughts can become ingrained, reinforcing a cycle of overthinking and self-limitation. By understanding the impact of negative thought patterns, we can begin to recognize their presence in our lives and take proactive steps to release them.

Recognizing negative thought patterns:

The first step in releasing negative thought patterns is to develop awareness and recognize when we are engaging in them. Negative thought patterns may include self-criticism, excessive worry, catastrophizing, or constant comparison to others. By paying attention to our thoughts and observing the patterns that arise, we can gain insight into our habitual thinking and begin the process of letting go.

Challenging negative thoughts:

Once we become aware of negative thought patterns, we can challenge their validity and replace them with more positive and empowering thoughts. This process involves questioning the evidence behind our negative thoughts and reframing them in a more realistic and constructive light. By actively challenging negative thoughts, we can break free from their influence and cultivate a more optimistic and balanced mindset.

Practicing mindfulness and detachment:

Mindfulness plays a vital role in releasing negative thought patterns. By practicing mindfulness, we develop the ability to observe our thoughts without getting caught up in them or attaching undue importance to them. This sense of detachment allows us to let go of negative thoughts more easily, recognizing them as passing mental events rather than absolute truths. Through mindfulness, we cultivate a greater sense of inner peace and resilience in the face of negative thinking.

Using visualization and imagery techniques:

Visualization and imagery techniques can be powerful tools for releasing negative thought patterns. By creating vivid mental images of letting go, we can symbolically release negative thoughts and emotions. For example, we might imagine placing our negative thoughts in a balloon and letting it float away, or visualizing them dissolving into a clear, peaceful stream. Through these techniques, we reinforce the intention to let go and create space for more positive and uplifting thoughts.

Journaling and expressive writing:

Journaling and expressive writing can provide a safe and cathartic outlet for releasing negative thought patterns. By putting our thoughts and emotions into words, we gain clarity and perspective. We can write about our worries, fears, and self-doubts, allowing them to be expressed and acknowledged. Through this process, we can gain insight, challenge negative beliefs, and create space for new and empowering thoughts to emerge.

Engaging in physical and emotional release:

Physical and emotional release practices can be effective in letting go of negative thought patterns. Engaging in activities such as yoga, tai chi, or dance can help release tension and promote a sense of flow and mindfulness. Additionally, practices like deep breathing exercises, progressive muscle relaxation, or engaging in hobbies and creative pursuits can channel our energy and focus away from negative thinking, promoting a sense of release and well-being.

Cultivating self-compassion and forgiveness:

Self-compassion and forgiveness are essential aspects of letting go of negative thought patterns. By cultivating self-compassion, we offer ourselves kindness and understanding when negative thoughts arise. We recognize that we are human and that everyone experiences negative thoughts from time to time. Instead of judging ourselves harshly, we treat ourselves with compassion, offering reassurance and support.

Forgiveness is another crucial aspect of releasing negative thought patterns. It involves letting go of grudges, resentments, and self-blame. By forgiving ourselves and others, we release the emotional baggage associated with negative thoughts and create space for healing and growth.

Practicing gratitude and positive affirmations:

Gratitude and positive affirmations are powerful tools for shifting our focus from negative to positive. By actively practicing gratitude, we cultivate a sense of appreciation for the present moment and acknowledge the blessings in our lives. This practice helps counteract negative thought patterns by redirecting our attention to the positive aspects of our experiences.

Positive affirmations involve consciously choosing and repeating positive statements about ourselves and our abilities. By affirming our strengths, worth, and potential, we rewire our thought patterns and create a more positive and empowering self-perception.

Setting boundaries and practicing self-care:

Setting boundaries and practicing self-care are essential for releasing negative thought patterns. Overthinking often arises from overwhelm and a lack of self-care. By setting healthy boundaries, we prioritize our well-being and create space for self-reflection, relaxation, and rejuvenation. This allows us to recharge and approach challenges with a clearer and more balanced mindset.

Engaging in activities that bring joy and fulfillment:

Engaging in activities that bring joy and fulfillment can help us release negative thought patterns. When we immerse ourselves in activities that we enjoy and are passionate about, we shift our focus away from overthinking and towards experiences that bring us happiness and fulfillment. By pursuing hobbies, spending time with loved ones, or pursuing personal interests, we create a positive and meaningful life that naturally counteracts negative thinking.

Seeking support:

Releasing negative thought patterns can be challenging, and seeking support from others can be immensely helpful. Whether it's talking to a trusted friend, joining a support group, or seeking professional guidance, reaching out to others can provide perspective, validation, and encouragement. By sharing our thoughts and feelings with others, we gain insights and support that assist us in letting go of negative thought patterns.

Conclusion:

In this chapter, we explored the art of letting go and strategies for releasing negative thought patterns. By recognizing negative thought patterns, challenging them, and practicing mindfulness and detachment, we can begin to release their hold on our minds. Visualization, journaling, physical and emotional release, self-compassion, and forgiveness are powerful practices that aid in the process of letting go. Additionally, gratitude, positive affirmations, setting boundaries, engaging in joyful activities, and seeking support all contribute to the release of negative thought patterns. Remember, releasing negative thought patterns is an ongoing process that requires self-awareness, commitment, and practice. By cultivating the art of letting go, we create space for positive thinking, personal growth, and a more peaceful and balanced mindset.

Chapter 7: Journaling techniques for clarity and emotional release.

———

I ntroduction:

In this chapter, we explore the power of journaling as a tool for gaining clarity, processing emotions, and promoting overall well-being. Journaling is a creative and therapeutic practice that allows us to express our thoughts, feelings, and experiences in a safe and private space. Through various journaling techniques, we can tap into our inner wisdom, release pent-up emotions, and gain a deeper understanding of ourselves. In this chapter, we will explore different journaling techniques that can help us achieve clarity and emotional release.

Stream of consciousness writing:

Stream of consciousness writing involves allowing our thoughts to flow freely onto the pages without judgment or censorship. This technique encourages us to write continuously, without pausing or editing our words. By letting our thoughts spill onto the pages, we can access subconscious thoughts and gain insights into our inner world. Stream of consciousness writing can help us identify patterns, uncover hidden emotions, and gain clarity on various aspects of our lives.

Gratitude journaling:

Gratitude journaling involves writing down things we are grateful for on a regular basis. This practice shifts our focus from negative to positive, as we intentionally reflect on the blessings and positive experiences in our lives. By cultivating a mindset of gratitude, we train our minds to notice and appreciate the goodness that surrounds us. Gratitude journaling can uplift our spirits, improve our overall outlook on life, and help us release negative emotions by shifting our attention to the positive.

Reflective journaling:

Reflective journaling is a practice that involves reflecting on past experiences, events, or interactions. It allows us to gain insight, learn from our experiences, and gain a deeper understanding of ourselves. Reflective journaling prompts may include questions like "What did I learn from this experience?" or "How did this situation make me feel?" By engaging in reflective journaling, we can process emotions, gain clarity, and identify areas for personal growth.

Emotional release journaling:

Emotional release journaling provides a safe space to express and release pent-up emotions. This technique involves writing about our emotions, allowing ourselves to fully experience and express them on the pages. It can involve venting, writing unsent letters, or simply describing our feelings in detail. By giving voice to our emotions through writing, we can release emotional tension, gain a sense of relief, and promote emotional well-being.

Future self journaling:

Future self journaling involves writing from the perspective of our future selves, imagining who we want to become and the life we want to lead. This technique allows us to explore our goals, dreams, and aspirations, and create a roadmap for our future. By writing about our ideal future and the steps we can take to get there, we gain clarity, motivation, and a sense of purpose. Future self journaling helps us release limiting beliefs and empowers us to take action towards our desired future.

Problem-solving journaling:

Problem-solving journaling is a technique that involves using journaling to explore solutions to challenges or problems we are facing. By writing about the problem, brainstorming possible solutions, and evaluating their pros and cons, we can tap into our creativity and problem-solving abilities. Problem-solving journaling allows us to gain clarity, consider different perspectives, and develop action plans to overcome obstacles.

Affirmation journaling:

Affirmation journaling involves writing positive affirmations about ourselves, our abilities, and our worth. By regularly affirming our strengths and positive qualities, we can reprogram our subconscious mind and cultivate a more positive self-image. Affirmation journaling helps us release self-doubt, boost self-confidence, and foster self-compassion.

Conclusion:

Journaling is a powerful practice for gaining clarity and emotional release. Through techniques like stream of consciousness writing, gratitude journaling, reflective journaling, emotional release journaling, future self journaling, problem-solving journaling, and affirmation journaling, we can tap into our inner thoughts and emotions, gain insights, and promote personal growth.

Journaling provides a safe and nonjudgmental space to explore our thoughts and feelings. It allows us to release pent-up emotions, process challenging experiences, and gain a deeper understanding of ourselves. By regularly engaging in journaling, we develop a stronger connection to our inner selves and can navigate life with more clarity and purpose.

One of the benefits of journaling is that it helps us become more self-aware. As we put our thoughts and emotions into words, we become more attuned to our inner landscape. This self-awareness allows us to identify patterns, triggers, and recurring thoughts or emotions that may be holding us back. By shining a light on these aspects of ourselves through journaling, we can make conscious choices to release negative patterns and cultivate positive ones.

Journaling also serves as a tool for emotional release. Sometimes we may find it difficult to express our emotions verbally or to share them with others. Journaling provides a safe outlet to pour out our feelings onto the pages. By writing about our emotions, we can validate and acknowledge them, allowing them to be felt and expressed. This process can bring a sense of relief, release emotional tension, and promote emotional well-being.

Furthermore, journaling allows us to gain clarity and perspective on various aspects of our lives. By reflecting on past experiences, exploring future possibilities, or seeking solutions to challenges, we can gain insights and new perspectives. Through the act of writing, we engage different parts of our brain and tap into our creative problem-solving abilities. This helps us find clarity and make informed decisions in our lives.

Journaling can also be a source of empowerment and self-compassion. By writing down our goals, dreams, and aspirations, we solidify our intentions and commit to taking action. We can use journaling to celebrate our successes, acknowledge our progress, and express self-compassion during challenging times. Through positive affirmations and self-encouragement, we reinforce our self-belief and build resilience.

In conclusion, journaling is a transformative practice that can bring clarity, emotional release, and personal growth. By engaging in various journaling techniques, we can explore our thoughts and feelings, gain insights, and develop a deeper connection with ourselves. Whether it's stream of consciousness writing, gratitude journaling, reflective journaling, emotional release journaling, future self journaling, problem-solving journaling, or affirmation journaling, each technique offers a unique approach to journaling for clarity and emotional well-being. Incorporating journaling into our daily or weekly routine can support our overall mental and emotional health, helping us navigate life with more ease and self-awareness.

Chapter 8: The role of gratitude in breaking free from overthinking.

———

Introduction:

In this chapter, we explore the powerful role of gratitude in breaking free from overthinking. Gratitude is a practice that involves intentionally acknowledging and appreciating the positive aspects of our lives. It is a transformative mindset that can shift our focus from overthinking and negative thought patterns to a more positive and optimistic outlook. In this chapter, we will delve into the benefits of gratitude and explore practical strategies for cultivating gratitude to overcome overthinking.

The power of gratitude:

Gratitude is more than just saying "thank you" or expressing appreciation for something. It is a mindset and a way of life that can profoundly impact our well-being. Research has shown that practicing gratitude regularly can have numerous positive effects on our mental and emotional health.

Shifting focus:

Overthinking often keeps us stuck in a cycle of negative thoughts and worries. Gratitude acts as a powerful antidote by shifting our focus to the positive aspects of our lives. When we intentionally focus on what we are grateful for, we redirect our attention away from overthinking and cultivate a more optimistic perspective.

Cultivating resilience:

Gratitude helps us develop resilience in the face of challenges and setbacks. By acknowledging the things we are grateful for, even in difficult times, we build a foundation of strength and hope. This mindset shift allows us to approach obstacles with a more positive mindset, enabling us to bounce back and find solutions more effectively.

Enhancing well-being:

Practicing gratitude has been linked to increased levels of happiness and life satisfaction. When we regularly express gratitude, we train our minds to notice and appreciate the good things in our lives, no matter how small. This sense of appreciation and contentment contributes to overall well-being and helps counteract the negative effects of overthinking.

Reducing stress:

Overthinking is often accompanied by stress and anxiety. Gratitude has been found to reduce stress levels by promoting a state of relaxation and contentment. When we focus on the things we are grateful for, we activate the parasympathetic nervous system, which helps calm the body and mind. This can help alleviate the stress and overwhelm that often accompany overthinking.

Practical strategies for cultivating gratitude:

Gratitude journaling:

Keeping a gratitude journal is a popular and effective way to cultivate gratitude. Set aside a few minutes each day to write down three to five things you are grateful for. It can be as simple as a beautiful sunset, a supportive friend, or a delicious meal. Writing them down helps solidify the positive experiences in your mind and reinforces a gratitude mindset.

Gratitude meditation:

Meditation is a powerful tool for cultivating gratitude. Find a quiet and comfortable space, close your eyes, and focus on your breath. With each inhale and exhale, bring to mind something you are grateful for. Allow the feeling of gratitude to fill your entire being. You can also visualize sending gratitude to specific people or situations. This practice helps deepen your sense of appreciation and gratitude.

Gratitude letters:

Take the time to write letters of gratitude to people who have positively impacted your life. Express your appreciation and let them know how grateful you are for their presence or actions. This not only cultivates gratitude within yourself but also strengthens your relationships and spreads positivity to others.

Gratitude walks:

Go for a walk in nature and intentionally focus on the things you are grateful for. Observe the beauty around you—the vibrant colors, the sounds of birds, or the gentle breeze. Allow yourself to fully immerse in the present moment and feel gratitude for the wonders of nature.

Gratitude rituals:

Create daily or weekly gratitude rituals that align with your preferences. It could be starting each day by mentally listing three things you are grateful for, or ending each day by reflecting on the positive moments and experiences you encountered. You can also incorporate gratitude into mealtime by saying a few words of appreciation before eating. These rituals serve as reminders to cultivate gratitude and bring awareness to the blessings in your life.

Gratitude jar:

Set up a gratitude jar in your home or office. Whenever something positive or noteworthy happens, write it down on a small piece of paper and place it in the jar. Over time, the jar will fill up with reminders of the good things that have happened. Whenever you're feeling overwhelmed or caught up in overthinking, take a moment to read a few notes from the jar and feel a sense of gratitude and positivity.

Gratitude partners:

Find a gratitude partner or create a gratitude group with friends or family members. Set a regular time to meet or connect and share what you are grateful for. By sharing and hearing others' gratitude, you not only deepen your own appreciation but also create a supportive and uplifting community focused on positivity.

Mindful gratitude:

Incorporate gratitude into your daily mindfulness practice. As you engage in activities like eating, showering, or walking, bring your attention to the present moment and consciously appreciate the experiences. Notice the taste and texture of the food, the sensation of water on your skin, or the rhythm of your footsteps. By infusing these moments with gratitude, you enhance your mindfulness practice and cultivate a deeper sense of appreciation.

Conclusion:

Gratitude is a powerful practice that can help break free from the trap of overthinking. By intentionally cultivating gratitude, we shift our focus from negativity to positivity, develop resilience, enhance our well-being, and reduce stress. Through gratitude journaling, meditation, gratitude letters, walks, rituals, and sharing with others, we can integrate gratitude into our daily lives and experience its transformative effects.

By embracing a gratitude mindset, we create a shift in our perception and open ourselves to the abundance of blessings that surround us. Gratitude allows us to appreciate the present moment, find joy in simple pleasures, and overcome the tendency to dwell on negative thoughts. It empowers us to break free from the overthinking cycle and embrace a more positive and fulfilling life.

As you continue on your journey of breaking free from overthinking, remember the power of gratitude as a tool for transformation. Practice gratitude consistently, and you will witness its profound impact on your mental and emotional well-being. Embrace the beauty of gratitude and let it guide you towards a life filled with joy, positivity, and clarity.

Chapter 9: Creating a supportive environment for mental clarity.

———

Introduction:

In this chapter, we explore the importance of creating a supportive environment for mental clarity. Our surroundings have a significant impact on our thoughts, emotions, and overall well-being. By intentionally designing an environment that fosters mental clarity and supports our efforts to overcome overthinking, we can create a space that promotes peace, focus, and productivity. In this chapter, we will delve into practical strategies for creating a supportive environment that nurtures mental clarity.

Declutter and organize:

Clutter and disorganization can contribute to mental clutter and overwhelm. Start by decluttering your physical space, removing any unnecessary items, and organizing your belongings. A clean and tidy environment promotes a sense of calm and clarity. Create designated spaces for different activities, such as a dedicated workspace for productivity or a serene corner for relaxation. Keep surfaces clear and free of distractions to foster mental clarity and focus.

Establish a daily routine:

Having a structured daily routine provides a sense of stability and reduces decision fatigue. Set consistent wake-up and bedtime routines to regulate your sleep patterns. Plan your day in advance, scheduling time for work, relaxation, exercise, and self-care. A well-structured routine helps minimize distractions and provides a clear roadmap for the day, allowing you to focus on tasks without getting overwhelmed by overthinking.

Designate a digital detox space:

In today's digital age, constant exposure to screens and notifications can contribute to overstimulation and mental clutter. Create a designated digital detox space in your home—a place where you can disconnect from technology and engage in activities that promote mental clarity. It could be a cozy reading nook, a meditation corner, or a peaceful outdoor area. Use this space to engage in offline activities like reading, journaling, or practicing mindfulness.

Surround yourself with inspirational elements:

Decorate your environment with elements that inspire and uplift you. Hang motivational quotes, artwork, or photographs that bring you joy and remind you of your goals and aspirations. Choose colors that promote a sense of calm and tranquility, such as soft blues or earthy tones. Surrounding yourself with positive and inspiring elements helps create a supportive atmosphere that encourages mental clarity and focus.

Incorporate nature:

Nature has a profound impact on our well-being and mental clarity. If possible, bring elements of nature into your environment. Open windows to let in fresh air and natural light. Add plants and flowers to your space, which not only beautify the surroundings but also purify the air and create a sense of calm. If you have access to outdoor space, create a peaceful retreat where you can connect with nature—a garden, a balcony, or a nearby park. Spending time in nature rejuvenates the mind and promotes mental clarity.

Minimize distractions:

Identify and minimize distractions in your environment that contribute to overthinking. Reduce background noise by using noise-canceling headphones or playing calming music. Turn off notifications on your phone or set specific times for checking emails and social media. Create boundaries to protect your focus and create a space that allows you to engage in deep work and meaningful activities without constant interruptions.

Foster supportive relationships:

Surround yourself with supportive and positive individuals who uplift and encourage you. Cultivate relationships with people who understand your goals and aspirations, and who support your journey to overcome overthinking. Engage in meaningful conversations, seek guidance, and share your challenges and victories. A supportive network provides emotional support, different perspectives, and accountability, all of which contribute to mental clarity and personal growth.

Prioritize self-care:

Make self-care a priority in your environment. Set aside time for activities that nourish your mind, body, and soul. Create a self-care corner with items such as scented candles, soothing music, comfortable seating, and items that bring you joy and relaxation. Use this space to engage in self-care practices like meditation, yoga, reading, or taking a relaxing bath. Prioritizing self-care in your environment creates a nurturing space where you can recharge, reduce stress, and cultivate mental clarity.

Seek supportive tools and resources:

Explore tools and resources that can support your journey of overcoming overthinking. This could include books, podcasts, or online courses focused on stress relief, mindfulness, and personal development. Fill your environment with these resources to inspire and guide you on your path towards mental clarity. Utilize technology apps that promote mindfulness, meditation, and productivity to enhance your daily routine and keep you on track.

Regularly evaluate and adjust:

Creating a supportive environment for mental clarity is an ongoing process. Regularly evaluate your surroundings and assess whether they continue to align with your goals and needs. Be open to making adjustments and refinements as necessary. As you grow and evolve, your environment should evolve with you, reflecting your changing priorities and aspirations.

Conclusion:

Creating a supportive environment for mental clarity is a vital aspect of overcoming overthinking. By intentionally designing our surroundings to promote peace, focus, and productivity, we can enhance our overall well-being and cultivate a mindset of clarity and calm. From decluttering and organizing to incorporating nature, minimizing distractions, fostering supportive relationships, and prioritizing self-care, there are numerous strategies to create a nurturing environment that supports our journey towards mental clarity.

Remember that your environment has a profound impact on your thoughts, emotions, and actions. By implementing the strategies outlined in this chapter and adapting them to your unique circumstances, you can create a space that nurtures mental clarity, reduces overthinking, and promotes overall well-being. Embrace the power of your surroundings and harness it as a tool for personal growth, productivity, and inner peace.

Chapter 10: Nurturing healthy relationships and boundaries.

———

I ntroduction:

In this chapter, we explore the importance of nurturing healthy relationships and setting boundaries as a means to overcome overthinking. Our relationships with others greatly impact our mental and emotional well-being. By fostering healthy connections and establishing clear boundaries, we can create supportive environments that promote peace, self-care, and a reduction in overthinking. In this chapter, we will delve into practical strategies for nurturing healthy relationships and setting boundaries to support our journey towards mental clarity.

Reflect on relationship dynamics:

Take time to reflect on the dynamics of your relationships. Consider how certain relationships contribute to or exacerbate overthinking. Are there individuals who consistently trigger negative thoughts or emotional distress? Are there patterns of codependency or unhealthy communication? Reflecting on these dynamics helps you gain clarity on the relationships that may need adjustment or healthier boundaries.

Communicate openly and assertively:

Effective communication is key to nurturing healthy relationships and setting boundaries. Express your thoughts, feelings, and needs clearly and assertively, while also being open to listening to others. Use "i" statements to express how you feel and communicate your boundaries in a respectful manner. Honest and open communication establishes a foundation of trust and mutual understanding.

Identify and honor your needs:

Understanding your own needs is essential for setting healthy boundaries. Take time to identify what you need in your relationships—whether it's space, support, respect, or emotional validation. Recognize that it is okay to prioritize your well-being and communicate these needs to others. Nurturing healthy relationships requires acknowledging and honoring your own needs.

Establish boundaries:

Boundaries serve as guidelines for how we engage with others and protect our well-being. Set clear boundaries in your relationships by defining what is acceptable and respectful behavior for you. This may involve establishing limits on the time and energy you invest in certain relationships or expressing your boundaries around sensitive topics. Boundaries provide a framework for healthier interactions and help prevent overthinking triggered by relationship stress.

Practice active listening:

Developing active listening skills fosters healthy communication and deeper connections with others. Be fully present when engaging in conversations, giving your undivided attention and suspending judgment. Seek to understand the perspectives and experiences of others, validating their feelings and opinions. Active listening promotes empathy, strengthens relationships, and reduces misunderstandings that can contribute to overthinking.

Cultivate supportive relationships:

Surround yourself with individuals who support your growth, well-being, and journey towards mental clarity. Seek out relationships built on mutual respect, trust, and positivity. Surrounding yourself with supportive friends, family, or mentors provides a network of encouragement, understanding, and constructive feedback. These relationships nurture your self-esteem and contribute to a more positive mindset.

Practice self-compassion:

Nurturing healthy relationships begins with cultivating self-compassion. Treat yourself with kindness, understanding, and forgiveness. Acknowledge that it's normal to make mistakes or have moments of overthinking. Embrace self-care practices that nourish your mind, body, and soul, and prioritize your own well-being. By practicing self-compassion, you create a foundation of self-love and resilience that enhances your relationships with others.

Assess and adjust relationships:

Regularly assess your relationships and determine whether they align with your values, goals, and well-being. It's important to recognize when certain relationships may be toxic or draining, contributing to overthinking. Assess whether the balance of give and take is healthy and if there is reciprocity in the support and care provided. Be willing to make adjustments, whether that involves setting firmer boundaries, seeking professional support, or considering whether a relationship is no longer serving your well-being.

Seek professional support:

Sometimes, nurturing healthy relationships and establishing boundaries may require professional support. If you find yourself struggling with maintaining healthy relationships or setting boundaries, consider seeking guidance from a therapist, counselor, or relationship coach. These professionals can provide valuable insights, tools, and strategies to help you navigate challenging dynamics, communicate effectively, and establish boundaries that promote your well-being.

Practice forgiveness and letting go:

Forgiveness is a powerful tool in nurturing healthy relationships and freeing ourselves from overthinking. Holding onto grudges and past hurts only perpetuates negative thought patterns and hinders personal growth. Practice forgiveness, both towards others and yourself, as a means of releasing the emotional burden that can contribute to overthinking. Letting go of resentment and embracing forgiveness creates space for healing and cultivating healthy relationships.

Conclusion:

Nurturing healthy relationships and setting boundaries is essential for overcoming overthinking and fostering mental clarity. By reflecting on relationship dynamics, practicing effective communication, identifying and honoring your needs, establishing clear boundaries, and cultivating supportive connections, you create an environment that supports your well-being and reduces overthinking triggers. Remember to practice active listening, cultivate self-compassion, assess and adjust relationships as needed, and seek professional support when necessary.

Embrace the journey of nurturing healthy relationships and setting boundaries as a means to enhance your overall well-being. As you prioritize your mental clarity and establish healthier dynamics, you create space for growth, fulfillment, and deeper connections with others. By fostering supportive relationships and maintaining clear boundaries, you empower yourself to overcome overthinking and live a more balanced and fulfilling life.

Chapter 11: Effective time management to reduce overthinking.

———

I ntroduction:

In this chapter, we explore the importance of effective time management in reducing overthinking. Time is a valuable resource, and how we utilize it greatly impacts our mental well-being. By managing our time effectively, we can create a sense of control, reduce overwhelm, and minimize the opportunities for overthinking to take hold. In this chapter, we will delve into practical strategies for mastering time management to foster mental clarity and break free from the cycle of overthinking.

Set clear goals and priorities:

Start by setting clear goals and identifying your priorities. What do you want to achieve? What tasks or activities are most important to you? Having a clear sense of direction allows you to allocate your time and energy accordingly, reducing the chances of getting caught up in overthinking about what you should be doing.

Break tasks into manageable chunks:

Large tasks or projects can be overwhelming and lead to overthinking. Break them down into smaller, manageable chunks. Create a step-by-step plan or to-do list that outlines the specific actions needed to accomplish each task. By focusing on one step at a time, you can avoid feeling overwhelmed and stay productive.

Utilize time-blocking techniques:

Time-blocking involves scheduling specific blocks of time for different tasks or activities. Assign dedicated time slots for work, relaxation, self-care, and other priorities. This technique helps you stay focused, prevents multitasking, and provides a clear structure for your day. By adhering to a set schedule, you minimize the chances of overthinking about how to best utilize your time.

Practice the 80/20 rule:

The 80/20 rule, also known as the Pareto Principle, states that roughly 80% of your results come from 20% of your efforts. Identify the tasks or activities that yield the most significant outcomes and focus your time and energy on those. By prioritizing the most impactful tasks, you can maximize your productivity and reduce the likelihood of overthinking about less important matters.

Avoid procrastination:

Procrastination often leads to increased stress and overthinking. Develop strategies to overcome procrastination, such as breaking tasks into smaller steps, setting deadlines, or using productivity techniques like the Pomodoro Technique (working in focused bursts with short breaks). By tackling tasks promptly and avoiding unnecessary delays, you prevent overthinking about unfinished or looming tasks.

Practice time awareness:

Develop a sense of time awareness by regularly checking in with yourself and assessing how you are spending your time. Are you allocating your time in alignment with your goals and priorities? Are there any time-wasting activities or distractions that could be minimized? By cultivating time awareness, you can make conscious choices about how you invest your time and reduce overthinking about wasted or unproductive hours.

Delegate and outsource:

Recognize that you don't have to do everything yourself. Delegate tasks to others when possible or consider outsourcing certain responsibilities. Whether it's at work or in your personal life, redistributing tasks can alleviate overwhelm and allow you to focus on activities that align with your strengths and priorities.

Practice time-bound decision making:

Avoid overthinking by implementing time-bound decision-making. Set deadlines for yourself when faced with choices or tasks. Give yourself a reasonable amount of time to gather information, weigh options, and make a decision. By imposing time limits, you prevent excessive rumination and empower yourself to move forward with confidence.

Take regular breaks:

Taking regular breaks throughout the day is crucial for maintaining focus and preventing mental exhaustion. Incorporate short breaks into your schedule to recharge and rejuvenate. Engage in activities that help clear your mind, such as going for a walk, practicing deep breathing, or engaging in mindfulness exercises. These breaks provide an opportunity to step away from tasks and give your mind a chance to rest, reducing the likelihood of overthinking.

Learn to say no:

One of the most effective time management strategies is learning to say no. Recognize that your time and energy are valuable resources, and it's important to protect them. Be selective about the commitments you take on and don't hesitate to decline requests or opportunities that don't align with your goals or priorities. Setting boundaries and saying no when necessary allows you to maintain control over your time and avoid overstretching yourself.

Practice time-management techniques:

Explore various time-management techniques and find what works best for you. Some popular techniques include the Eisenhower Matrix (prioritizing tasks based on urgency and importance), the ABC Method (assigning tasks with letters to indicate priority), or the Two-Minute Rule (tackling tasks that can be completed in two minutes immediately). Experiment with different approaches and adapt them to your unique needs and preferences.

Minimize distractions:

Identify and minimize distractions that can lead to overthinking and time wastage. Create a conducive environment for focus by turning off notifications on your devices, setting aside dedicated workspaces, and utilizing productivity tools that block or limit access to distracting websites or apps. By reducing distractions, you create a space that promotes concentration and minimizes the chances of getting caught up in overthinking.

Regularly review and adjust:

Effective time management requires periodic evaluation and adjustments. Take time to review how you are managing your time and identify areas for improvement. Reflect on what strategies are working well and what could be modified. Be open to adapting your approach as needed to optimize your productivity and reduce overthinking.

Practice self-reflection:

Engage in regular self-reflection to gain insights into your time management habits and patterns. Ask yourself questions such as: What time of day am I most productive? Are there specific tasks or activities that consistently lead to overthinking? What strategies have been effective in managing my time? Self-reflection helps you identify areas for growth and refine your time management practices.

Celebrate progress and achievements:

Acknowledge and celebrate your progress and achievements along the way. Recognize the value of effectively managing your time and the positive impact it has on your well-being. By celebrating milestones, both big and small, you reinforce positive habits and motivate yourself to continue practicing effective time management.

Conclusion:

Effective time management is a powerful tool in reducing overthinking and fostering mental clarity. By setting clear goals, breaking tasks into manageable chunks, utilizing time-blocking techniques, and avoiding procrastination, you can take control of your time and minimize the opportunities for overthinking to arise. Remember to practice time awareness, delegate when possible, and learn to say no to protect your valuable resources.

Through consistent practice and reflection, you can cultivate a balanced and productive approach to managing your time, leading to increased mental clarity and reduced overthinking. Embrace the strategies outlined in this chapter, adapt them to your unique circumstances, and enjoy the benefits of effective time management in your journey towards a more fulfilling and focused life.

Chapter 12: Embracing imperfection and letting go of perfectionism.

―――

I ntroduction:

In this chapter, we explore the concept of embracing imperfection and letting go of perfectionism as a means to overcome overthinking. Perfectionism can be a relentless pursuit of flawlessness that often leads to self-criticism, anxiety, and excessive rumination. By embracing imperfection and releasing the need for perfection, we can reduce overthinking, cultivate self-compassion, and create a healthier mindset. In this chapter, we will delve into practical strategies for embracing imperfection and letting go of perfectionism to foster mental clarity and well-being.

Recognize the illusion of perfection:

Perfectionism often stems from a belief that perfection is attainable and necessary for success or happiness. Begin by recognizing that perfection is an illusion. No one is flawless, and striving for perfection only sets unrealistic expectations. Embrace the idea that imperfections and mistakes are natural and part of the learning and growth process.

Challenge negative self-talk:

Perfectionism is fueled by negative self-talk and self-criticism. Become aware of your inner dialogue and challenge negative thoughts and beliefs. Replace self-critical statements with more compassionate and realistic ones. Practice self-encouragement and remind yourself that making mistakes and having imperfections is part of being human.

Set realistic standards:

Reevaluate your standards and expectations. Set realistic goals and standards for yourself that take into account your abilities, limitations, and the circumstances at hand. Avoid setting impossibly high standards that only serve to fuel overthinking and dissatisfaction. Aim for progress rather than perfection.

Focus on effort and growth:

Shift your focus from the end result to the effort and growth that comes from the process. Embrace a growth mindset, where mistakes and setbacks are viewed as opportunities for learning and improvement. Celebrate the progress you make along the way, rather than solely focusing on the final outcome.

Practice self-compassion:

Cultivate self-compassion as a counter to perfectionism. Treat yourself with kindness, understanding, and acceptance. Be gentle with yourself when faced with setbacks or mistakes. Practice self-care and self-soothing techniques to nurture your emotional well-being. Self-compassion allows you to let go of self-judgment and reduce overthinking about perceived shortcomings.

Embrace the beauty of imperfection:

Recognize the beauty and uniqueness in imperfection. Imperfections make us human and add depth and character to our lives. Embrace the quirks, flaws, and idiosyncrasies that make you who you are. Appreciate the imperfect aspects of your journey and find joy in the imperfections of others.

Cultivate a growth-oriented mindset:

Adopt a growth-oriented mindset that focuses on continuous learning and improvement. Embrace challenges as opportunities to expand your skills and knowledge. Emphasize the process of growth rather than fixating on achieving perfection. By cultivating a growth-oriented mindset, you can reduce overthinking and embrace the journey of self-development.

Practice mindfulness:

Incorporate mindfulness practices into your daily life to help you stay present and centered. Mindfulness allows you to observe your thoughts and emotions without judgment, reducing the tendency to get caught up in overthinking. By practicing mindfulness, you develop a greater sense of acceptance and peace with yourself and the world around you.

Embrace mistakes as learning opportunities:

Shift your perspective on mistakes. Instead of viewing them as failures or reasons for self-criticism, see them as valuable learning opportunities. Mistakes provide insights, teach us resilience, and offer chances for personal growth. Embrace the lessons learned from your mistakes and let go of overthinking about what went wrong.

Surround yourself with supportive people:

Surround yourself with individuals who support and encourage your journey of embracing imperfection. Seek out friends, family members, or support groups that promote self-acceptance and provide a safe space for vulnerability. Connecting with others who share similar struggles can help you feel understood and reinforce the importance of letting go of perfectionism.

Practice self-reflection:

Engage in regular self-reflection to gain deeper insights into your perfectionistic tendencies and their impact on your well-being. Take time to assess how perfectionism manifests in different areas of your life and how it contributes to overthinking. Reflect on the benefits of embracing imperfection and the negative consequences of striving for unattainable standards.

Challenge perfectionistic behaviors:

Identify specific behaviors associated with perfectionism and challenge them. For example, if you tend to excessively edit and revise your work, set a limit on the number of revisions you allow yourself. If you have a fear of making mistakes, intentionally engage in activities where mistakes are inevitable and practice accepting them with grace. By confronting perfectionistic behaviors, you gradually reduce their hold over your thoughts and actions.

Celebrate imperfect moments:

Intentionally seek out and celebrate imperfect moments in your life. Embrace situations where things didn't go according to plan but still brought valuable experiences or lessons. Whether it's trying a new hobby, exploring unfamiliar territory, or engaging in creative endeavors, celebrate the beauty of imperfection and the joy that can be found in unexpected outcomes.

Practice letting go:

Letting go is a powerful practice in breaking free from perfectionism and overthinking. Release the need to control every outcome and accept that some things are beyond your influence. Practice mindfulness-based techniques, such as meditation or deep breathing, to cultivate a sense of surrender and detachment from perfectionistic tendencies.

Focus on the process, not the outcome:

Shift your focus from solely fixating on the end result to appreciating and enjoying the process. Embrace the journey of growth, learning, and self-discovery that occurs along the way. By immersing yourself in the present moment and engaging wholeheartedly in the process, you reduce the mental burden of overthinking about attaining perfection.

Engage in creative expression:

Creativity provides a wonderful outlet for embracing imperfection. Engage in creative activities such as painting, writing, dancing, or playing music. Allow yourself to express freely without worrying about the outcome being flawless. Embrace the beauty of imperfections in your creative endeavors and let go of any self-imposed expectations of perfection.

Practice gratitude:

Cultivate a sense of gratitude for the imperfections in your life. Recognize that imperfections often lead to unexpected blessings, personal growth, and deeper connections with others. Take time each day to reflect on the things you appreciate, including both the perfect and imperfect aspects of your life. Gratitude helps shift your focus towards acceptance and contentment.

Seek professional support:

If perfectionism and overthinking continue to significantly impact your well-being, consider seeking professional support. A therapist or counselor can provide guidance, tools, and strategies to help you navigate and overcome perfectionistic tendencies. They can assist you in developing healthy coping mechanisms and cultivating a mindset that embraces imperfection.

Conclusion:

Embracing imperfection and letting go of perfectionism is a transformative journey that requires self-reflection, self-compassion, and a willingness to challenge ingrained beliefs and behaviors. By recognizing the illusion of perfection, setting realistic standards, and focusing on growth and effort, you can reduce overthinking and cultivate a healthier mindset.

Through mindfulness, self-acceptance, and surrounding yourself with supportive individuals, you can break free from the shackles of perfectionism and embrace the beauty of imper

Chapter 13: Harnessing the power of visualization for mental clarity.

———

Introduction:

In this chapter, we explore the power of visualization as a tool for achieving mental clarity and reducing overthinking. Visualization is the practice of creating vivid mental images or scenarios to evoke specific feelings, sensations, or outcomes. By harnessing the power of visualization, we can train our minds to focus on positive thoughts, enhance our ability to solve problems, and cultivate a sense of calm and clarity. In this chapter, we will delve into the techniques and benefits of visualization and provide practical guidance on incorporating it into your daily life.

Understanding visualization:

Visualization involves using your imagination to create detailed mental images or scenarios. It is a form of mental rehearsal that helps your mind and body respond as if the imagined scenario were real. Visualization can be used to achieve various goals, including reducing stress, enhancing performance, boosting confidence, and gaining mental clarity. By engaging your senses and emotions in the visualization process, you activate the power of your mind to bring about positive change.

Setting clear intentions:

Before engaging in visualization, it is important to set clear intentions. Clarify what you want to achieve or the specific outcome you desire. Whether it's finding clarity on a particular issue, making a decision, or overcoming obstacles, having a clear intention provides a focus for your visualization practice. Write down your intentions to reinforce them in your mind and establish a sense of purpose.

Creating a relaxing environment:

Find a quiet and comfortable space where you can engage in visualization without distractions. Create an environment that promotes relaxation, such as dimming the lights, playing soft music, or using aromatherapy. The goal is to create a soothing ambiance that allows you to fully immerse yourself in the visualization process.

Developing a visualization script:

Craft a script or narrative that guides your visualization practice. Describe the desired scenario or outcome in detail, incorporating sensory and emotional elements. For example, if you are visualizing a peaceful beach scene, describe the sound of waves, the warmth of the sun on your skin, and the smell of the ocean breeze. Tailor the script to your specific goals and preferences, making it as vivid and engaging as possible.

Engaging the senses:

During visualization, engage all your senses to make the experience more immersive and impactful. Visualize colors, shapes, and textures. Imagine the sounds, smells, and tastes associated with the scenario. By activating your senses, you strengthen the neural connections in your brain and make the visualization more realistic and powerful.

Incorporating emotional connection:

Tap into the emotions associated with your desired outcome during visualization. Imagine how it would feel to experience the mental clarity, calmness, and confidence you seek. Embrace the positive emotions that arise as you visualize the desired scenario. This emotional connection adds depth and authenticity to your visualization practice.

Practicing regularly:

Consistency is key when harnessing the power of visualization. Make it a habit to engage in visualization exercises regularly. Set aside dedicated time each day to immerse yourself in the practice. As with any skill, the more you practice, the more proficient you become at using visualization for mental clarity.

Combining visualization with relaxation techniques:

Enhance the effectiveness of visualization by combining it with relaxation techniques. Prior to visualization, engage in deep breathing exercises, progressive muscle relaxation, or meditation to calm your mind and body. Relaxation techniques help create a receptive state for visualization and deepen your overall sense of mental clarity and focus.

Applying visualization to problem-solving:

Visualization can be a valuable tool for problem-solving and decision-making. When faced with a complex issue, visualize different scenarios and outcomes. Imagine yourself successfully overcoming obstacles, finding creative solutions, or making confident decisions. By visualizing positive outcomes and engaging in the process of problem-solving, you stimulate your brain's creative thinking and problem-solving abilities. Visualization helps you explore different perspectives and possibilities, allowing you to approach challenges with clarity and confidence.

Using guided visualization:

If you find it challenging to create your own visualization scripts or maintain focus during visualization, you can utilize guided visualization resources. Guided visualizations are pre-recorded or written scripts that provide step-by-step instructions to lead you through the visualization process. These resources often incorporate soothing background music and calming narration, making it easier to relax and immerse yourself in the visualization experience.

Visualizing positive affirmations:

Combine visualization with positive affirmations to enhance its effectiveness. As you visualize your desired outcome, incorporate affirmations that reinforce your intentions and affirm your capabilities. Repeat positive statements such as

"I am clear, focused, and confident," or "I trust my intuition and make decisions with ease." By combining visualization with affirmations, you strengthen the positive mindset necessary for mental clarity.

Applying visualization to future goal achievement:

Visualization can also be a powerful tool for manifesting your future goals. Imagine yourself successfully achieving your goals, whether it's excelling in your career, building fulfilling relationships, or realizing personal growth. Visualize the steps you need to take, the challenges you may face, and the ultimate fulfillment of your aspirations. By consistently visualizing your desired future, you reinforce your motivation, clarify your path, and align your actions with your goals.

Embracing flexibility in visualization:

While visualization is a structured practice, it is essential to embrace flexibility and adapt it to your unique needs and preferences. Experiment with different visualization techniques, adapt scripts to align with your goals, and modify the duration of your visualization sessions. The key is to find an approach that resonates with you and feels natural and effective.

Reflecting on your visualization experiences:

After each visualization session, take a few moments to reflect on your experience. Journaling about your visualizations can help deepen your understanding of the insights, emotions, or clarity that arise during the practice. Reflecting allows you to integrate the benefits of visualization into your daily life and gain valuable self-awareness.

Integrating visualization into daily life:

Extend the benefits of visualization beyond dedicated practice sessions by incorporating it into your daily life. Take a few moments during your day to visualize a peaceful scene, imagine a successful outcome, or visualize yourself confidently navigating a challenging situation. By integrating brief visualizations into your routine, you reinforce mental clarity, reduce overthinking, and maintain a positive mindset.

Conclusion:

Harnessing the power of visualization is a valuable tool for achieving mental clarity, reducing overthinking, and aligning your actions with your desired outcomes. By setting clear intentions, engaging your senses and emotions, practicing regularly, and combining visualization with relaxation techniques, you can experience the transformative effects of visualization in your life. Embrace the practice of visualization and unlock its potential to bring about mental clarity, confidence, and success.

Chapter 14: Unleashing creativity as a pathway to overcome overthinking.

———

I ntroduction:

In this chapter, we explore the transformative power of creativity as a pathway to overcome overthinking. Creativity is a fundamental aspect of human nature that allows us to express ourselves, solve problems, and connect with our inner selves. By tapping into our creative potential, we can break free from the cycle of overthinking and discover new perspectives, solutions, and a sense of flow. In this chapter, we will delve into the techniques and benefits of unleashing creativity and provide practical guidance on incorporating it into your life to overcome overthinking.

Understanding creativity:

Creativity is not limited to artistic pursuits; it encompasses a broad range of activities and forms of expression. It is the ability to generate new ideas, perspectives, and solutions. Embracing creativity involves stepping outside of familiar patterns, embracing uncertainty, and allowing yourself to explore new possibilities. By adopting a creative mindset, you can cultivate a sense of freedom, curiosity, and playfulness that counteracts the grip of overthinking.

Embracing the creative process:

The creative process is a journey that involves ideation, exploration, experimentation, and iteration. It is essential to embrace each stage of the creative process and let go of expectations of perfection or immediate results. By embracing the process, you create space for innovative ideas to emerge and free yourself from the constraints of overthinking.

Engaging in creative activities:

Engage in creative activities that resonate with your interests and passions. Whether it's painting, writing, dancing, playing music, cooking, or gardening, find activities that allow you to express yourself freely and without judgment. The goal is to immerse yourself in the creative process, letting go of overthinking and tapping into your innate creativity.

Embracing playfulness:

Cultivate a sense of playfulness in your creative endeavors. Playfulness removes the pressure of perfection and encourages exploration and experimentation. Approach your creative activities with a childlike curiosity, embracing the joy of discovery and the freedom to make mistakes. By infusing playfulness into your creative process, you invite spontaneity, fresh perspectives, and breakthrough moments.

Breaking routine:

Step out of your comfort zone and break free from routine to stimulate your creativity. Explore new environments, try new experiences, and expose yourself to different cultures, arts, and perspectives. By exposing yourself to diverse influences, you broaden your creative palette and open up new possibilities for innovative thinking.

Embracing mistakes and failure:

Shift your perspective on mistakes and failure, viewing them as valuable learning opportunities rather than setbacks. Embracing a growth mindset allows you to approach creative endeavors with resilience and a willingness to learn from setbacks. By reframing mistakes as stepping stones on the path to success, you diminish the fear of failure and liberate yourself from overthinking.

Engaging in divergent thinking:

Divergent thinking is the ability to generate multiple ideas, solutions, or perspectives. Practice divergent thinking by engaging in brainstorming sessions or mind mapping exercises. Challenge yourself to come up with as many ideas as possible without judgment or self-censorship. Divergent thinking opens up new possibilities and helps break free from the narrow focus of overthinking.

Cultivating mindfulness:

Incorporate mindfulness practices into your creative process. Mindfulness involves being fully present and aware of the current moment, without judgment. By cultivating mindfulness, you can quiet the incessant chatter of overthinking and create a space for creative insights to arise. Engage in mindfulness meditation, deep breathing exercises, or simply immersing yourself fully in the creative activity at hand.

Seeking inspiration:

Expose yourself to sources of inspiration that fuel your creative fire. Surround yourself with art, literature, music, and other forms of creative expression that resonate with you. Visit art galleries, attend concerts or performances, read books, and engage with other creatives in your community. Seeking inspiration not only stimulates your own creativity but also provides fresh perspectives and ideas that can help you overcome overthinking.

Embracing collaboration:

Collaboration with others can be a powerful catalyst for creativity. Engage in creative collaborations with like-minded individuals or join creative groups and communities. Collaborative projects allow you to tap into collective wisdom, share ideas, and spark innovative thinking. The synergy of collaboration can help break through the barriers of overthinking and lead to breakthrough moments of creativity.

Creating a creative space:

Designate a space in your home or workspace that is dedicated to your creative pursuits. This space should be free from distractions and filled with materials, tools, and resources that inspire and support your creative process. By creating a physical space that nurtures your creativity, you signal to your mind and body that it's time to unleash your creative potential.

Incorporating creative rituals:

Develop rituals or routines that signal the beginning of your creative practice. These rituals can be as simple as lighting a candle, playing specific music, or reciting affirmations. By establishing consistent creative rituals, you create a sense of anticipation and focus that helps you overcome overthinking and enter a state of creative flow.

Embracing solitude:

Allow yourself periods of solitude to recharge and connect with your inner self. Solitude provides the space for introspection, reflection, and incubation of ideas. Disconnect from external distractions and create dedicated time for quiet contemplation, journaling, or simply being alone with your thoughts. Solitude nurtures your creativity and allows you to tap into your deepest insights and inspirations.

Balancing structure and freedom:

Strike a balance between structure and freedom in your creative pursuits. While structure provides a framework and discipline for your creative process, allowing for focus and progress, freedom allows for exploration, experimentation, and spontaneity. Find a balance that works for you, honoring the need for structure to combat overthinking while also embracing the freedom to express and explore.

Celebrating your creative achievements:

Celebrate your creative achievements, no matter how big or small. Acknowledge and appreciate the progress you've made, the challenges you've overcome, and the unique contributions you've made through your creativity. Celebrating your creative achievements boosts your confidence, reinforces your creative mindset, and motivates you to continue overcoming overthinking and embracing your creative potential.

Conclusion:

Unleashing creativity is a powerful pathway to overcome overthinking and tap into your innate potential for innovation, self-expression, and problem-solving. By embracing the creative process, embracing playfulness, breaking routine, and cultivating a growth mindset, you can liberate yourself from the shackles of overthinking and embark on a journey of creative discovery. Embrace your creativity, trust your unique perspective, and allow your creative spirit to guide you towards mental clarity and self-expression.

Chapter 15: Mindful decision-making strategies for mental clarity.

———

Introduction:

In this chapter, we explore mindful decision-making strategies as a powerful tool for cultivating mental clarity. The decisions we make shape our lives, yet the process of decision-making can often be clouded by overthinking, doubt, and external influences. By incorporating mindfulness into our decision-making process, we can navigate the complexities of choices with greater awareness, intentionality, and peace of mind. In this chapter, we will delve into practical strategies and techniques to foster mindful decision-making and enhance our mental clarity.

Cultivating present-moment awareness:

Begin by grounding yourself in the present moment before making decisions. Take a few deep breaths, bring your attention to your body and senses, and let go of distractions. By cultivating present-moment awareness, you create a foundation of clarity and focus from which to approach your decision-making process.

Clarifying your values and priorities:

Before making a decision, take time to reflect on your core values and priorities. What truly matters to you? What are your long-term goals and aspirations? Aligning your decisions with your values and priorities ensures that your choices are in harmony with your authentic self, reducing the potential for regrets or internal conflicts.

Practicing non-attachment:

Let go of attachments to specific outcomes or expectations. Recognize that life is fluid, and outcomes may differ from what we envision. By practicing non-attachment, you free yourself from excessive worrying and overthinking about the potential consequences of your decisions. Instead, focus on the process and trust that the right path will unfold.

Engaging reflective thinking:

Engage in reflective thinking to gain insight into your decision-making process. Set aside time for introspection and journaling, allowing yourself to explore your thoughts, feelings, and motivations surrounding the decision at hand. Reflective thinking helps uncover underlying biases, fears, and assumptions, leading to more informed and mindful choices.

Considering multiple perspectives:

Expand your perspective by considering various viewpoints and opinions. Seek feedback from trusted friends, mentors, or experts who can offer insights or alternative angles on the decision. This practice broadens your understanding of the situation and helps you make more informed and balanced choices.

Trusting your intuition:

Tap into your intuition, that inner wisdom that arises beyond logical analysis. Pay attention to your gut feelings, hunches, or subtle nudges when making decisions. Your intuition often holds valuable insights that can guide you towards the best course of action. Trusting your intuition empowers you to make decisions with confidence and clarity.

Applying the cost-benefit analysis:

Conduct a cost-benefit analysis to evaluate the potential risks, benefits, and consequences of each option. Assess both short-term and long-term impacts on various aspects of your life, such as relationships, finances, career, and personal well-being. This analysis provides a structured framework for weighing the pros and cons of different choices.

Practicing mindful deliberation:

Engage in mindful deliberation by bringing focused attention to the decision-making process. Notice any mental chatter, biases, or emotional reactions that may arise. Observe your thoughts and emotions without judgment and return to the present moment when distractions arise. Mindful deliberation cultivates clarity, objectivity, and a deeper understanding of the decision at hand.

Embracing the power of "no":

Learn to say "no" when necessary to align your choices with your priorities and boundaries. Setting healthy boundaries and being selective in your commitments helps prevent overwhelm, stress, and regret. Embracing the power of "no" allows you to make decisions with greater intention and authenticity.

Considering long-term consequences:

Look beyond immediate gratification and consider the long-term consequences of your decisions. Think about how each choice may impact your future well-being, relationships, and personal growth. Consider the potential ripple effects and the alignment of your decision with your long-term goals and aspirations. Taking a holistic and future-oriented perspective enables you to make decisions that support your overall life vision.

Embracing the middle way:

Avoid extremes and embrace the middle way when making decisions. Extremes often lead to imbalance and unnecessary stress. Strive for moderation, finding a balanced approach that considers different aspects of the decision and seeks harmony between competing interests. Embracing the middle way fosters equanimity and prevents overthinking and analysis paralysis.

Engaging in contemplative practices:

Incorporate contemplative practices, such as meditation or mindfulness exercises, into your decision-making process. These practices quiet the mind, enhance self-awareness, and facilitate clarity. Taking a few moments of stillness and introspection before making a decision allows you to access your inner wisdom and make choices from a place of calmness and presence.

Recognizing decision fatigue:

Be aware of decision fatigue and its impact on your mental clarity. Our ability to make sound decisions diminishes as we exhaust our cognitive resources. When faced with numerous decisions, prioritize and simplify whenever possible. Delegate non-essential choices, create routines, and reduce unnecessary options to conserve mental energy for more critical decisions.

Seeking external support:

If you feel overwhelmed or indecisive, seek support from trusted mentors, coaches, or therapists. Engaging in conversations with objective and experienced individuals can provide valuable insights, guidance, and a fresh perspective. Their input can help you gain clarity and navigate complex decisions with greater confidence.

Embracing the learning opportunity:

Approach decision-making as an ongoing learning opportunity rather than a quest for perfection. Embrace the idea that some decisions may not yield the desired outcome, but they can offer valuable lessons and growth opportunities. Embracing the learning process reduces the fear of making mistakes and allows you to approach decisions with a growth mindset.

Conclusion:

Mindful decision-making is a transformative practice that cultivates mental clarity, intentionality, and peace of mind. By incorporating present-moment awareness, reflective thinking, multiple perspectives, and trust in your intuition, you can navigate decisions with greater confidence and authenticity. Remember that decision-making is not about achieving perfection but rather making choices aligned with your values, priorities, and long-term vision.

Embrace the power of mindful decision-making and experience the freedom and clarity that come from aligning your choices with your authentic self.

Chapter 16: Embracing self-care practices to calm an overactive mind.

———

I ntroduction:

In this chapter, we explore the importance of self-care practices in calming an overactive mind. In today's fast-paced world, we often find ourselves overwhelmed by stress, responsibilities, and constant mental chatter. Taking time to prioritize self-care allows us to nurture our mental, emotional, and physical well-being, leading to a calmer and more balanced state of mind. In this chapter, we will delve into various self-care practices that can help calm an overactive mind and promote inner peace and serenity.

Prioritizing rest and sleep:

One of the most fundamental self-care practices for calming an overactive mind is prioritizing rest and quality sleep. Create a consistent sleep routine, ensuring you get enough hours of sleep to recharge and rejuvenate your mind and body. Establish a relaxing bedtime ritual, such as reading a book, taking a warm bath, or practicing gentle stretching, to prepare your mind for a restful night's sleep.

Engaging in mindful movement:

Incorporate mindful movement practices, such as yoga, tai chi, or qigong, into your daily routine. These practices not only enhance physical well-being but also cultivate a sense of presence and inner calm. Focus on the sensations of your body, the rhythm of your breath, and the gentle flow of movement, allowing your mind to find stillness and release excessive mental activity.

Nurturing a daily meditation practice:

Commit to a daily meditation practice to calm and center your mind. Find a quiet space, sit comfortably, and bring your attention to the present moment. Choose a meditation technique that resonates with you, whether it's focused attention on the breath, loving-kindness meditation, or guided visualization. Regular meditation trains your mind to become more resilient, focused, and at peace, reducing overthinking and mental clutter.

Practicing deep breathing exercises:

Deep breathing exercises are simple yet powerful techniques for calming an overactive mind. Take slow, deep breaths, focusing on the sensation of the breath entering and leaving your body. Deep breathing triggers the relaxation response, activating the parasympathetic nervous system and reducing stress and anxiety. Incorporate deep breathing exercises into your daily routine or use them as a tool to regain mental clarity during moments of overwhelm.

Engaging in creative expression:

Expressing your creativity is a powerful self-care practice that can quiet an overactive mind. Engage in activities such as painting, writing, playing a musical instrument, or engaging in crafts. These creative outlets allow you to enter a state of flow, where time seems to disappear and the mind becomes focused and calm. Creative expression offers a therapeutic release and promotes mental clarity and emotional well-being.

Connecting with nature:

Spending time in nature is a rejuvenating self-care practice that helps quiet the noise of an overactive mind. Take walks in the park, hike in the mountains, or simply sit by a tranquil body of water. Nature has a calming effect on the mind, reducing stress and anxiety while promoting a sense of awe and wonder. Allow yourself to be fully present in nature, soaking in its beauty and finding solace in its serenity.

Cultivating healthy boundaries:

Setting healthy boundaries is crucial for self-care and maintaining mental clarity. Learn to say "no" to excessive demands or commitments that drain your energy and contribute to overthinking. Prioritize your well-being and protect your time and energy by establishing clear boundaries with others. By honoring your needs and limitations, you create space for self-care and a quieter, more focused mind.

Engaging in mindful eating:

Practice mindful eating as a form of self-care for your body and mind. Slow down and savor each bite, paying attention to the flavors, textures, and sensations of the food. Engage all your senses in the experience of eating. By practicing mindful eating, you cultivate a deeper connection with your body and its needs, fostering a sense of balance and satisfaction. This mindful approach to nourishment can help calm an overactive mind by bringing focus and awareness to the present moment.

Establishing digital detoxes:

In today's digital age, constant exposure to screens and information overload can contribute to an overactive mind. Establish regular digital detoxes to give your mind a break from the constant stimulation. Designate specific times or days where you disconnect from electronic devices, social media, and emails. Instead, engage in activities that promote relaxation and mindfulness, such as reading a book, taking a nature walk, or spending quality time with loved ones.

Cultivating gratitude:

Practicing gratitude is a transformative self-care practice that shifts your focus from negative overthinking to appreciation and positivity. Take time each day to reflect on the things you are grateful for. It could be as simple as a beautiful sunset, a supportive friend, or a nourishing meal. Cultivating gratitude rewires your brain to notice and appreciate the good in life, fostering a sense of contentment and peace.

Engaging in stress-relieving activities:

Identify stress-relieving activities that bring you joy and relaxation, and make them a regular part of your self-care routine. It could be taking a bubble bath, practicing aromatherapy, listening to soothing music, or engaging in a hobby that brings you happiness. These activities help reduce stress hormones, quiet the mind, and create a sense of calm and well-being.

seeking support and connection:

Don't hesitate to seek support and connection when needed. Reach out to trusted friends, family members, or a therapist to share your thoughts and feelings. Sometimes, verbalizing our thoughts and emotions can help release mental tension and provide a fresh perspective. Engaging in meaningful conversations and nurturing connections with others can bring comfort and a sense of belonging.

Practicing self-compassion:

Be kind to yourself and practice self-compassion. Acknowledge that everyone experiences moments of overthinking, and it's okay to have a busy mind at times. Treat yourself with understanding, patience, and self-care during those moments. Practice self-compassionate self-talk and remind yourself that you are doing the best you can. Embracing self-compassion allows you to let go of self-judgment and cultivate a more peaceful relationship with your thoughts.

Establishing a relaxation routine:

Create a relaxation routine that incorporates various calming activities. It could include a combination of meditation, gentle stretching, breathing exercises, or listening to calming music. Dedicate a specific time each day or week to engage in these practices, allowing your mind to unwind, relax, and find balance. Consistency in your relaxation routine reinforces its effectiveness in calming an overactive mind.

Engaging in journaling:

Journaling is a powerful self-care practice that can help calm an overactive mind. Set aside regular time for journaling to express your thoughts, fears, and worries on paper. This process helps release mental clutter, gain clarity, and develop self-awareness. You can also use journaling to explore positive affirmations, gratitude lists, or creative writing exercises that promote relaxation and mental clarity.

Conclusion:

Embracing self-care practices is essential for calming an overactive mind and cultivating inner peace. By prioritizing rest, engaging in mindful movement, nurturing a daily meditation practice, and incorporating various self-care activities into your routine, you can create a sanctuary of calm within yourself. Remember that self-care is a continuous journey of self-discovery and self-nurturing. Find what works best for you and make self-care a non-negotiable part of your life.

Self-care practices help you recharge, restore balance, and create space for mental clarity. By taking care of your physical, emotional, and mental well-being, you enhance your ability to navigate life's challenges with a calmer and more focused mind.

Incorporate the self-care practices mentioned in this chapter into your daily life. Prioritize restful sleep, engage in mindful movement, and establish a regular meditation practice. Make time for activities that bring you joy and help you relax, such as creative expression, connecting with nature, and practicing gratitude.

It's also important to set boundaries and establish digital detoxes to give your mind a break from constant stimulation. Seek support and connection from loved ones or professionals when needed, and practice self-compassion during moments of overthinking.

Remember that self-care is not selfish but essential for your overall well-being. By taking care of yourself, you are better equipped to show up fully in all areas of your life, including work, relationships, and personal growth.

Commit to embracing self-care as a lifelong practice. Continuously explore new activities and techniques that resonate with you, as self-care is a deeply personal journey. Adapt your self-care routine as needed and make it a priority, even during busy and challenging times.

In conclusion, by embracing self-care practices, you can calm an overactive mind and create a foundation of mental clarity and well-being. Nurture yourself, prioritize your needs, and cultivate a sense of balance and peace. Remember, self-care is not an indulgence but a necessary investment in your overall health and happiness.

Chapter 17: Strategies for overcoming analysis paralysis.

———

I ntroduction:

In this chapter, we delve into the topic of analysis paralysis—a state of overthinking and indecision that often hinders our progress and keeps us stuck in a cycle of inaction. Many of us have experienced moments when we become overwhelmed by the sheer amount of information, options, and possibilities, making it challenging to make a decision. In this chapter, we explore effective strategies for overcoming analysis paralysis and regaining our ability to make confident choices.

Define your priorities:

Start by clarifying your priorities and goals. Take the time to reflect on what truly matters to you and what you hope to achieve. When you have a clear understanding of your priorities, it becomes easier to filter out unnecessary information and focus on what is most relevant to your decision-making process.

Set a deadline:

Establishing a deadline for making a decision can be incredibly helpful in overcoming analysis paralysis. Deadlines create a sense of urgency and force you to take action. Set a realistic timeframe for yourself and commit to making a decision within that time frame. This time constraint can help prevent excessive rumination and encourage you to weigh the pros and cons more efficiently.

Limit your options:

Having too many options can often lead to analysis paralysis. Instead, narrow down your choices to a manageable number. Consider the essential factors and criteria for your decision and eliminate options that do not align with your priorities. By reducing the number of choices, you can focus your energy on evaluating the remaining options more effectively.

Gather relevant information:

While it's crucial not to get overwhelmed by an abundance of information, gathering relevant and necessary information is essential for informed decision-making. Identify the key pieces of information that will contribute to your decision and seek them out deliberately. Be selective in your research, focusing on reliable sources and experts in the field. This targeted approach will prevent information overload and provide you with the necessary insights to make an informed choice.

Use decision-making frameworks:

Utilize decision-making frameworks to guide your thought process and organize your analysis. There are various frameworks available, such as the pros and cons list, decision trees, or SWOT analysis (Strengths, Weaknesses, Opportunities, Threats). These frameworks provide structure and help you evaluate different factors systematically. Select a framework that aligns with your decision and apply it to gain clarity and facilitate the decision-making process.

Trust your intuition:

Sometimes, excessive analysis can lead to disregarding our intuition, which can be a valuable guide in decision-making. Pay attention to your gut feelings and instincts. While it's essential to gather information and weigh the facts, also listen to your inner voice. Trusting your intuition can lead to more confident decisions and a sense of alignment with your true desires.

Embrace imperfection:

Perfectionism often fuels analysis paralysis. Recognize that there is no such thing as a perfect decision and that taking action is more important than waiting for an ideal outcome. Embrace the concept of "good enough" and understand that mistakes and course corrections are a natural part of the decision-making process. Allow yourself to be flexible and adaptable, understanding that decisions can be adjusted as needed.

Break it down:

If you're feeling overwhelmed by a complex decision, break it down into smaller, manageable tasks or milestones. This approach helps you focus on one step at a time, making the process less daunting. By breaking the decision into smaller parts, you can make progress while reducing the pressure associated with making a single overwhelming choice.

Seek external input:

Don't hesitate to seek input from trusted friends, mentors, or experts who can provide a fresh perspective. Engaging in discussions and seeking different viewpoints can broaden your understanding and help you see the situation from new angles.

Practice decision-making:

Overcoming analysis paralysis requires practice. Engage in decision-making exercises to sharpen your skills and build confidence. Start with small decisions and gradually work your way up to more significant choices. By actively making decisions, you develop a sense of empowerment and learn to trust your judgment.

Emphasize action and learning:

Shift your focus from seeking the perfect decision to emphasizing action and learning. Understand that even if a decision doesn't turn out as expected, it provides valuable feedback and an opportunity for growth. Embrace a mindset of continuous learning and improvement, knowing that every decision is a stepping stone on your journey.

Manage fear of failure:

Fear of making the wrong decision often contributes to analysis paralysis. Recognize that failure is a natural part of life and an opportunity for growth. Embrace a growth mindset and view failures as learning experiences. Cultivate self-compassion and remind yourself that it's okay to make mistakes. Embracing the possibility of failure frees you from the paralyzing fear and allows you to move forward with more confidence.

Take breaks:

When faced with a particularly challenging decision, taking breaks can provide much-needed perspective and mental clarity. Step away from the decision-making process temporarily to engage in activities that relax and rejuvenate you. It could be going for a walk, practicing mindfulness, engaging in a hobby, or spending time with loved ones. These breaks recharge your mind and allow you to approach the decision with a fresh perspective.

Set boundaries for analysis:

While it's important to gather information and analyze options, set boundaries for how much time you allocate to analysis. Determine a specific timeframe for gathering information, conducting research, and evaluating options. Once the timeframe is up, make a conscious decision to move forward and take action. Setting boundaries prevents analysis from becoming a never-ending process and keeps you focused on making a decision.

Practice acceptance:

Accept that there is no guaranteed outcome or certainty in decision-making. Recognize that uncertainty is a natural part of life, and making decisions is an ongoing process. Let go of the need for absolute certainty and embrace the inherent uncertainty that accompanies decision-making. Cultivate a mindset of acceptance and trust in your ability to navigate the unknown.

Celebrate decision-making:

Acknowledge and celebrate the act of making a decision. Recognize that reaching a decision is an accomplishment in itself, regardless of the outcome. Reward yourself for taking action and moving forward. Celebrating decision-making reinforces positive behavior and helps overcome the fear and hesitancy associated with analysis paralysis.

Conclusion:

Overcoming analysis paralysis is a skill that can be developed with practice and conscious effort. By defining priorities, setting deadlines, gathering relevant information, trusting your intuition, and embracing imperfection, you can break free from the cycle of overthinking and make confident decisions. Remember that decision-making is a dynamic process, and it's essential to approach it with a growth mindset and a willingness to learn. With these strategies in hand, you can overcome analysis paralysis and move forward with clarity and conviction.

Chapter 18: Tapping into intuition to reduce overthinking.

———

I ntroduction:

In this chapter, we explore the power of intuition and how it can help reduce overthinking. Intuition is the innate ability to understand or know something without the need for conscious reasoning. By learning to tap into our intuition, we can access a deeper level of wisdom and make decisions with greater ease and clarity. In this chapter, we will discuss techniques and practices that can help us connect with our intuition and overcome the tendency to overthink.

What is intuition?

Intuition is often described as a gut feeling, a hunch, or a sense of knowing that arises spontaneously. It is a subtle yet powerful inner guidance system that can provide insights and information beyond what our logical mind can comprehend. Intuition is not limited to a select few; it is a natural ability that exists within all of us.

Trusting your gut:

One of the first steps in tapping into intuition is learning to trust your gut. Pay attention to those initial feelings or sensations that arise when you are faced with a decision or a situation. Often, our intuition communicates through physical sensations in the body, such as a feeling of expansion or contraction. Practice trusting these intuitive signals and allowing them to guide your decision-making process.

Quiet the mind:

Overthinking can drown out the voice of intuition. To access your intuitive wisdom, it is important to quiet the noise of the mind. Engage in practices such as meditation, deep breathing, or mindfulness to calm the mental chatter.

Create moments of stillness and silence in your day-to-day life to create space for intuition to emerge.

Cultivate mindfulness:

Mindfulness is a powerful tool for connecting with intuition. By bringing focused attention to the present moment, you become more attuned to subtle cues and signals from your intuition. Practice mindfulness in daily activities, such as eating, walking, or engaging in conversations. By being fully present, you open yourself up to receiving intuitive guidance.

Listen to your body:

The body is a powerful instrument for accessing intuition. Pay attention to the physical sensations that arise when you are making decisions or contemplating a course of action. Notice if your body feels light and expansive or heavy and contracted. Your body's response can provide valuable insights into what aligns with your intuition.

Engage in creative practices:

Creativity and intuition are deeply connected. Engaging in creative practices, such as painting, writing, or dancing, can help bypass the analytical mind and tap into the intuitive realm. Allow yourself to explore and express your creativity without judgment or self-criticism. These creative endeavors can provide a direct pathway to accessing your intuition.

Journaling and reflection:

Journaling is a powerful tool for accessing and exploring your intuition. Set aside time for reflective writing, where you can freely express your thoughts, feelings, and insights. Use journaling prompts to delve deeper into specific questions or areas of concern. As you write, pay attention to any intuitive nudges or messages that come through.

Practice non-attachment:

Attachment to specific outcomes can cloud your intuition. When making decisions, practice non-attachment to a particular result and instead focus on aligning with your inner guidance. Trust that the right answer or solution will unfold in due time. Let go of the need to control every aspect and embrace the flow of life.

Seek solitude:

Spending time alone in solitude can create an environment conducive to connecting with your intuition. Take regular breaks from external stimuli and find moments of solitude where you can be with your thoughts and feelings. Engage in activities such as walking in nature, sitting in silence, or engaging in self-reflection. Solitude provides an opportunity to listen to the whispers of your intuition.

Act on intuition:

Tapping into intuition is not just about receiving insights; it also involves taking action based on that guidance. Trusting your intuition requires courage and a willingness to follow the wisdom that arises within you. Here are some strategies for acting on your intuition:

Start with small decisions: Begin by practicing with smaller, less consequential decisions. Notice the intuitive nudges that arise and act upon them, even if they seem contrary to your logical mind. As you gain confidence in your intuitive abilities, you can apply them to more significant decisions.

Test your intuition: When faced with a decision, try making a choice based on your intuition and see how it unfolds. Reflect on the outcomes and learn from them. Over time, you will develop a sense of which intuitive signals are accurate and reliable.

Embrace uncertainty: Following your intuition may sometimes lead you down an uncertain path. Embrace the unknown and trust that your intuition will guide you in the right direction. Embracing uncertainty allows you to expand your comfort zone and tap into new possibilities.

Reflect on past experiences: Look back at moments when you followed your intuition and how it served you well. Recall instances when you ignored your intuition and the consequences that followed. Reflecting on past experiences can strengthen your trust in your intuitive abilities and encourage you to act upon them.

Seek support: Surround yourself with individuals who honor and respect intuition. Engage in conversations with like-minded individuals who have experienced the power of intuition in their own lives. Sharing experiences and insights can provide validation and encouragement on your intuitive journey.

Learn from mistakes: It's important to remember that intuitive guidance is not foolproof. There may be times when your intuition leads you astray or when you misinterpret the signals. View these experiences as opportunities for growth and learning. Adjust your approach, refine your understanding of your intuitive cues, and continue to develop your relationship with your intuition.

Conclusion:

Tapping into intuition is a powerful way to reduce overthinking and gain clarity in decision-making. By learning to trust your gut, quieting the mind, cultivating mindfulness, listening to your body, engaging in creative practices, journaling, practicing non-attachment, seeking solitude, and acting on your intuition, you can develop a strong connection to your intuitive wisdom. Embracing your intuition allows you to navigate life with greater ease, confidence, and authenticity. Trust yourself, listen to the whispers of your intuition, and embrace the transformative power it holds.

Chapter 19: Mindful communication for enhanced mental clarity.

Introduction:

Effective communication plays a crucial role in our daily lives, impacting our relationships, work, and overall well-being. However, in the midst of our busy lives, we often engage in communication without fully being present, leading to misunderstandings, conflicts, and increased mental clutter. In this chapter, we explore the practice of mindful communication as a powerful tool for enhancing mental clarity and fostering healthier connections with others. By cultivating awareness and intentionality in our communication, we can promote understanding, empathy, and meaningful connections.

The power of mindful communication:

Mindful communication involves being fully present and engaged in our interactions with others. It requires attentive listening, non-judgmental observation, and clear expression. By practicing mindful communication, we can reduce misunderstandings, improve relationships, and create a more harmonious and supportive environment.

Cultivating presence:

To engage in mindful communication, it is essential to cultivate presence. This means being fully present in the moment, letting go of distractions, and giving our undivided attention to the person or people we are communicating with. By being present, we can better understand and respond to the nuances of the conversation, fostering deeper connections and mutual understanding.

Active listening:

Active listening is a fundamental aspect of mindful communication. It involves listening with full attention, without interrupting or formulating responses in our minds. Practice giving space for the speaker to express themselves fully before responding. This deep level of listening allows us to truly understand the speaker's perspective and respond in a more thoughtful and compassionate manner.

Non-verbal communication:

Mindful communication extends beyond words. Pay attention to your non-verbal cues, such as facial expressions, body language, and tone of voice. Be aware of the messages you are conveying through these non-verbal signals and strive to align them with your intended message. Similarly, observe the non-verbal cues of others, as they can provide valuable insights into their emotions and thoughts.

Choosing words mindfully:

The words we choose have a significant impact on the clarity and effectiveness of our communication. Practice choosing words mindfully, considering their impact and ensuring they accurately convey your intended message. Be aware of the tone and delivery of your words, aiming for a compassionate and respectful approach. Mindful word choice fosters understanding, prevents misunderstandings, and promotes constructive dialogue.

Responding, not reacting:

Mindful communication involves responding rather than reacting. Instead of impulsively reacting to a statement or situation, take a moment to pause and reflect before responding. This pause allows you to consider the best way to communicate your thoughts and feelings, promoting more thoughtful and effective communication.

Empathy and compassion:

Empathy and compassion are essential qualities in mindful communication. Strive to understand others' perspectives, validate their emotions, and respond with empathy and kindness. Cultivating empathy and compassion creates a safe and supportive space for open and honest communication, enhancing mental clarity and strengthening relationships.

Mindful conflict resolution:

Conflicts are a natural part of human interaction, but mindful communication can help navigate them more effectively. When faced with conflict, practice active listening, validate the emotions of all parties involved, and express your thoughts and feelings with clarity and compassion. Aim for a solution-oriented approach that considers the needs and perspectives of everyone involved.

Setting boundaries:

Mindful communication also involves setting boundaries. Be aware of your limits and communicate them assertively and respectfully. Setting boundaries fosters healthy communication dynamics, promotes self-care, and prevents mental clutter that may arise from overcommitting or neglecting personal needs.

Reflecting on communication:

Regularly reflect on your communication patterns and experiences. Consider the effectiveness of your communication, areas for improvement, and moments where mindful communication has positively impacted your mental clarity and relationships. Reflecting on your communication allows you to identify any patterns of overthinking, miscommunication, or missed opportunities for mindful connection. Use these reflections as learning opportunities to refine your communication skills and deepen your commitment to mindful communication.

Mindful communication in digital spaces:

In today's digital age, mindful communication is equally important in virtual environments. Whether through emails, text messages, or online platforms, apply the principles of mindful communication to your digital interactions. Take the time to read and understand messages before responding, choose your words carefully, and be mindful of tone and context. Mindful communication in digital spaces helps prevent misunderstandings and promotes meaningful connections.

Practicing mindful silence:

Silence has its own power in communication. Embrace mindful silence as a way to process information, show respect, and create space for deeper understanding. In conversations, allow pauses for reflection or to give others an opportunity to speak. Mindful silence fosters a more balanced and harmonious communication dynamic.

Mindful communication in challenging situations:

Challenging situations can put our communication skills to the test. During moments of conflict, stress, or tension, practice mindful communication even more consciously. Take deep breaths, ground yourself in the present moment, and strive to respond with clarity and compassion. Mindful communication in challenging situations can help diffuse tensions, promote understanding, and prevent further escalation.

The practice of loving-kindness:

Incorporating loving-kindness into your communication enhances the mindful aspect of your interactions. Before engaging in conversations, silently offer well-wishes or positive intentions to the other person. This practice creates a foundation of goodwill and empathy, setting a positive tone for the communication exchange.

Continuous learning and growth:

Mindful communication is a lifelong practice that requires continuous learning and growth. Stay open to feedback from others, as well as self-reflection, to identify areas for improvement. Engage in workshops, courses, or reading materials that explore effective communication techniques and deepen your understanding of mindful communication. The more you invest in your communication skills, the more you will enhance your mental clarity and strengthen your relationships.

Conclusion:

Mindful communication is a transformative practice that enhances our mental clarity and enriches our connections with others. By cultivating presence, active listening, conscious word choice, empathy, and compassion, we create an environment of understanding and respect. Mindful communication allows us to navigate conflicts with grace, foster deeper connections, and reduce mental clutter caused by overthinking or miscommunication. Embrace the power of mindful communication and experience the positive impact it has on your overall well-being.

Chapter 20: The role of exercise and movement in overcoming overthinking.

―――――

I ntroduction:

Physical exercise and movement play a significant role in our overall well-being, including our mental health. In this chapter, we explore the powerful impact of exercise and movement on overcoming overthinking. Engaging in regular physical activity not only benefits our physical health but also has profound effects on our mental clarity, stress reduction, and emotional well-being. By understanding the connection between exercise and overthinking, we can harness the transformative power of movement to break free from the cycle of excessive rumination and gain a greater sense of mental clarity and calm.

The mind-body connection:

The mind and body are deeply interconnected, and engaging in physical exercise helps promote a healthy balance between the two. When we exercise, our body releases endorphins, which are natural mood-boosting chemicals that promote feelings of happiness and well-being. This biochemical response positively influences our mental state, reducing anxiety, stress, and overthinking.

Stress reduction:

One of the key benefits of exercise in overcoming overthinking is its ability to reduce stress. Physical activity helps dissipate accumulated tension and releases built-up energy, allowing us to let go of racing thoughts and worries. Regular exercise has been shown to decrease levels of cortisol, the stress hormone, and increase the production of serotonin, a neurotransmitter associated with feelings of calm and contentment.

Improved cognitive function:

Engaging in exercise and movement has been linked to improved cognitive function, including enhanced focus, attention, and memory. When we exercise, blood flow to the brain increases, delivering oxygen and nutrients essential for optimal brain function. This improved cognitive function allows us to think more clearly, make decisions with greater ease, and maintain mental clarity.

Increased mindfulness:

Exercise provides an opportunity to cultivate mindfulness by immersing ourselves fully in the present moment. Whether it's through running, yoga, dancing, or any other form of physical activity, focusing on the sensations of our body and the rhythm of our movements anchors us in the present and helps quiet the incessant chatter of overthinking. Mindful movement allows us to shift our attention away from rumination and brings us into a state of flow and embodiment.

Enhancing emotional well-being:

Regular exercise is associated with enhanced emotional well-being and a reduction in symptoms of depression and anxiety. Physical activity stimulates the release of endorphins, which act as natural mood elevators. Additionally, exercise promotes the production of neurotransmitters like dopamine and norepinephrine, which are involved in regulating mood and promoting feelings of happiness and relaxation. Engaging in movement can be a powerful tool for managing and overcoming overthinking by promoting emotional balance and resilience.

Alternative perspective and problem-solving:

Physical exercise provides a break from our usual thought patterns and can offer a fresh perspective on the challenges we face. When we engage in movement, we shift our focus away from overthinking and create space for new ideas and insights to emerge. Exercise stimulates creativity, allowing us to approach problems from different angles and find innovative solutions.

Social connection and support:

Many forms of exercise and movement can be done in a social setting, such as group fitness classes, team sports, or outdoor activities. Engaging in physical activity with others fosters social connection and support, which can significantly contribute to our mental well-being. Social interaction during exercise provides a sense of belonging, reduces feelings of isolation, and offers opportunities for sharing experiences and support. This social connection helps alleviate overthinking by providing a supportive network and creating a sense of community.

Finding joy and self-care:

Exercise can be an enjoyable and fulfilling experience that brings joy and positivity into our lives. Engaging in activities that we genuinely enjoy promotes a sense of self-care and nurtures our overall well-being. When we prioritize regular exercise as part of our self-care routine, we send a powerful message to ourselves that our physical and mental well-being matter. By carving out time for movement and honoring our bodies, we reinforce the importance of self-care and create a positive feedback loop that supports our efforts to overcome overthinking.

Creating a balanced lifestyle:

Incorporating exercise and movement into our daily lives helps create a more balanced lifestyle. Overthinking often stems from an imbalance between mental and physical activities. By incorporating regular exercise, we counterbalance the mental strain of overthinking with physical activity, creating equilibrium within ourselves. This balance allows us to approach challenges and stressors with a clearer mind and a greater sense of resilience.

Sustainable exercise habits:

To reap the long-term benefits of exercise in overcoming overthinking, it's important to establish sustainable exercise habits. Find activities that you enjoy and that align with your preferences and lifestyle. Whether it's jogging, swimming, cycling, or practicing yoga, choose activities that you look forward to and that can be easily integrated into your routine. Consistency is key, so aim for a realistic and manageable exercise schedule that you can maintain over the long term.

Mindful movement practices:

In addition to traditional forms of exercise, there are various mindful movement practices that can further support our journey of overcoming overthinking. Practices like tai chi, qigong, and mindful walking emphasize the integration of movement, breath, and awareness. These practices not only enhance physical fitness but also cultivate mental clarity, relaxation, and a deep sense of presence.

Personalizing your exercise routine:

Each individual is unique, and what works for one person may not work for another. It's essential to personalize your exercise routine based on your preferences, fitness level, and any specific considerations or limitations you may have. Consulting with a healthcare professional or a certified fitness instructor can help you design a tailored exercise plan that suits your needs and supports your goals of overcoming overthinking.

Conclusion:

Exercise and movement are powerful allies in our journey to overcome overthinking and cultivate mental clarity. By understanding the role of physical activity in reducing stress, improving cognitive function, promoting mindfulness, enhancing emotional well-being, and fostering a balanced lifestyle, we can harness the transformative benefits of exercise. Integrating regular exercise into our lives allows us to break free from the cycle of overthinking, find solace in the present moment, and nurture our overall well-being. Embrace the power of movement and let it guide you towards a more peaceful and clear-minded existence.

Chapter 21: Strategies for handling uncertainty and overthinking the future.

———

I ntroduction:

Uncertainty about the future can be a significant source of overthinking and anxiety. In this chapter, we explore strategies for handling uncertainty and breaking free from the cycle of overthinking related to the future. By developing a resilient mindset and adopting practical tools, we can navigate uncertainty with greater clarity and peace of mind. These strategies empower us to embrace the present moment, let go of excessive worrying, and cultivate a positive and proactive approach to the future.

Embracing the reality of uncertainty:

The first step in handling uncertainty is accepting that it is an inevitable part of life. Recognize that no one has complete control over the future, and trying to predict or control every outcome is unrealistic. Embracing the reality of uncertainty allows you to shift your focus from trying to eliminate it to developing skills and strategies to navigate it effectively.

Cultivating mindfulness and present-moment awareness:

Practicing mindfulness and present-moment awareness is a powerful tool for managing overthinking about the future. By anchoring yourself in the present, you can redirect your attention away from anxious thoughts and concerns. Engaging in mindfulness practices such as meditation, deep breathing, or body scans can help you develop a non-judgmental awareness of the present moment and reduce overthinking about the future.

Developing a growth mindset:

Adopting a growth mindset enables you to view uncertainty as an opportunity for growth and learning rather than a threat. Embrace the belief that challenges and setbacks can be valuable lessons and stepping stones towards personal development. By reframing uncertainty as a catalyst for growth, you can shift your mindset from fear and overthinking to curiosity and resilience.

Setting realistic expectations:

When facing uncertainty, it's important to set realistic expectations for yourself and the future. Avoid placing excessive pressure on yourself to have all the answers or to achieve specific outcomes. Instead, focus on setting meaningful goals and taking small steps towards them. Embrace the journey of exploration and discovery, knowing that it's okay to adapt and adjust along the way.

Practicing self-compassion:

Uncertainty and overthinking can be emotionally challenging, so it's crucial to practice self-compassion. Be kind and understanding towards yourself when facing uncertainties, acknowledging that it's normal to feel anxious or uncertain. Treat yourself with the same empathy and support you would offer to a loved one going through a similar situation. Self-compassion helps alleviate the negative effects of overthinking and fosters a sense of inner peace and acceptance.

Engaging in strategic planning:

While it's essential to embrace uncertainty, it doesn't mean that planning and preparation are unnecessary. Engage in strategic planning by setting realistic goals, breaking them down into actionable steps, and creating a flexible roadmap for the future. This approach allows you to proactively address uncertainties while maintaining a sense of direction and purpose.

Seeking support and collaboration:

During times of uncertainty, seeking support from others can provide valuable perspectives and insights. Reach out to trusted friends, family members, or mentors who can offer guidance and support. Collaborating with others allows you to share the burden of overthinking and gain new perspectives that can help navigate uncertainty more effectively.

Engaging in problem-solving:

When faced with uncertainty, engage in problem-solving rather than dwelling on worst-case scenarios. Break down complex situations into manageable components, brainstorm potential solutions, and take action towards finding practical resolutions. Taking proactive steps to address uncertainties empowers you and helps alleviate overthinking by focusing your energy on constructive problem-solving.

Practicing gratitude:

Cultivating gratitude in the face of uncertainty helps shift your focus from what might go wrong to what is going well in your life. Regularly reflect on the things you are grateful for, even in uncertain times. This practice helps to counterbalance overthinking and anxiety by redirecting your attention to the positive aspects of your life. Write down or verbalize what you are grateful for each day, whether it's the support of loved ones, your health, or simple joys like a beautiful sunset or a good cup of coffee. Cultivating gratitude fosters a sense of resilience and helps you maintain a positive outlook even in the face of uncertainty.

Engaging in self-reflection:

Taking time for self-reflection allows you to gain clarity and perspective on your thoughts and emotions related to the future. Set aside dedicated moments to reflect on your aspirations, values, and priorities. Consider what truly matters to you and how you can align your actions with your desired future. Self-reflection provides a space for introspection and helps you make intentional decisions rather than getting caught up in overthinking.

Managing information consumption:

In the age of constant information and news updates, it's important to be mindful of your consumption habits. Limit exposure to excessive news or social media that may trigger overthinking and anxiety. Stay informed, but also create boundaries to protect your mental well-being. Choose reliable sources of information and allocate specific times to catch up on news, allowing yourself to stay informed without becoming overwhelmed by information overload.

Embracing flexibility and adaptability:

One of the keys to handling uncertainty is embracing flexibility and adaptability. Understand that plans may change, circumstances may shift, and unexpected challenges may arise. By adopting a flexible mindset, you can adapt to new situations, revise your plans when necessary, and find creative solutions to navigate uncertainty. Embracing flexibility allows you to let go of rigid expectations and reduces the tendency to overthink every potential outcome.

Engaging in relaxation techniques:

In times of uncertainty and overthinking, practicing relaxation techniques can help calm your mind and reduce anxiety. Explore techniques such as deep breathing exercises, progressive muscle relaxation, guided imagery, or mindfulness-based stress reduction. These practices promote relaxation, reduce tension, and enhance mental clarity. Incorporate them into your daily routine to create moments of calm amidst uncertainty.

Celebrating small victories:

Amidst uncertainty, it's important to acknowledge and celebrate your small victories and accomplishments. Recognize and appreciate the progress you have made, no matter how small it may seem. Celebrating these milestones boosts your confidence, reinforces positive thinking patterns, and counteracts the tendency to overthink and focus solely on future uncertainties.

Emphasizing self-care:

Prioritizing self-care is crucial when navigating uncertainty and overcoming overthinking. Take care of your physical, emotional, and mental well-being by engaging in activities that bring you joy and relaxation. Nurture yourself through healthy eating, regular exercise, sufficient sleep, and engaging in hobbies or activities that rejuvenate your spirit. Self-care replenishes your energy, strengthens resilience, and provides a solid foundation for managing uncertainty.

Conclusion:

Handling uncertainty and overcoming overthinking about the future requires a combination of mindset shifts, practical strategies, and self-care practices. By embracing the reality of uncertainty, cultivating mindfulness, setting realistic expectations, seeking support, and engaging in problem-solving, you can navigate uncertainty with more clarity and peace of mind. Remember to practice self-compassion, celebrate small victories, and prioritize self-care throughout your journey. With these strategies in place, you can break free from the cycle of overthinking and approach the future with confidence, resilience, and a positive mindset.

Chapter 22: Mindful eating for nourishment and clear thinking.

———

I ntroduction:

In our fast-paced and busy lives, we often overlook the importance of mindful eating. However, the way we eat has a significant impact on our overall well-being, including our mental clarity and ability to think clearly. In this chapter, we explore the concept of mindful eating and how it can support nourishment and clear thinking. By bringing awareness to our eating habits and making conscious choices, we can enhance our physical health, improve digestion, and cultivate a sense of mental clarity.

The basics of mindful eating:

Mindful eating involves paying attention to the entire experience of eating, from selecting food to chewing and savoring each bite. It emphasizes being present in the moment and engaging all of our senses while eating. By slowing down and fully experiencing our meals, we can develop a deeper connection with our bodies and the food we consume.

Developing awareness of hunger and fullness:

One aspect of mindful eating is tuning into our body's hunger and fullness cues. Rather than relying on external factors like the time of day or portion sizes, we learn to listen to our bodies and eat when we are genuinely hungry. Similarly, we practice stopping eating when we feel comfortably full, avoiding overeating or undereating. This awareness allows us to nourish our bodies optimally and prevent the discomfort and mental fog that can arise from extreme hunger or overindulgence.

Engaging the senses:

Mindful eating invites us to engage all our senses while eating. Take the time to appreciate the colors, textures, and aromas of your food. Notice the sound of each bite and savor the flavors as they unfold in your mouth. By fully immersing ourselves in the sensory experience of eating, we can enhance our enjoyment and satisfaction, leading to a more nourishing and fulfilling meal.

Eating with intention and gratitude:

Approaching meals with intention and gratitude can transform our eating experiences. Before each meal, take a moment to express gratitude for the nourishment in front of you. Reflect on the effort and resources that went into producing the food. This practice helps cultivate a sense of appreciation and mindfulness, allowing us to savor each bite with a deeper understanding of the nourishment it provides.

Mindful portion control:

Mindful eating involves being mindful of portion sizes and listening to our bodies' signals of fullness. Instead of relying on external measurements, we learn to trust our internal cues and eat until we feel satisfied, but not overly full. This practice helps us maintain a healthy relationship with food, preventing overconsumption and supporting optimal digestion and mental clarity.

Chewing and digestion:

The process of chewing is an essential aspect of mindful eating. Taking the time to thoroughly chew our food allows for better digestion and nutrient absorption. It also slows down the eating process, giving our bodies time to signal when we are full. By chewing mindfully, we can reduce digestive discomfort and promote clearer thinking by allowing our bodies to focus on digestion rather than feeling overwhelmed by a large, undigested meal.

Recognizing emotional eating:

Mindful eating encourages us to be aware of our emotions and how they can influence our eating habits. Emotional eating, where we turn to food for comfort or distraction, can lead to overeating and hinder mental clarity. By practicing mindfulness, we can recognize emotional triggers, find alternative ways to address our emotions, and develop healthier coping strategies.

Creating a peaceful eating environment:

The environment in which we eat plays a significant role in our eating experience and mental clarity. Create a calm and peaceful eating environment by minimizing distractions such as television, phones, or work-related activities. Instead, focus on creating a space that promotes relaxation and mindfulness, such as setting the table with care, lighting a candle, or playing soft background music. This intentional environment allows us to fully immerse ourselves in the present moment and engage in mindful eating practices.

Practicing mindful snacking:

Mindful eating is not limited to main meals; it can also be applied to snacks. Often, we consume snacks mindlessly, without paying attention to the quantity or quality of what we're eating. By practicing mindful snacking, we can bring awareness to our snack choices, savor each bite, and notice how the food makes us feel. This practice promotes a sense of satisfaction and prevents mindless overeating.

Exploring nutrient-dense foods:

Incorporating nutrient-dense foods into our meals supports both physical and mental well-being. These foods are rich in vitamins, minerals, and antioxidants that nourish our bodies and enhance brain function. By consciously choosing foods that provide essential nutrients, we can optimize our cognitive abilities, improve focus, and support clear thinking.

Cultivating mindful grocery shopping:

The practice of mindful eating extends beyond the act of eating itself. Mindful grocery shopping involves making conscious choices about the foods we bring into our homes. Take the time to read labels, select fresh produce, and choose whole foods that align with your health and well-being goals. By being intentional during the shopping process, we set ourselves up for success in practicing mindful eating at home.

Noticing the effects on mental clarity:

As you incorporate mindful eating practices into your daily life, pay attention to the effects on your mental clarity and overall well-being. Notice if you feel more focused, energized, or mentally sharp after practicing mindful eating. By developing this connection between your eating habits and mental clarity, you can reinforce the importance of mindful eating in your life.

Mindful eating as a form of self-care:

Engaging in mindful eating is an act of self-care. It allows us to nourish our bodies and minds in a way that promotes overall well-being. By prioritizing mindful eating, we show ourselves love and respect, recognizing that our bodies deserve to be nourished with intention and mindfulness.

Conclusion:

Mindful eating is a powerful practice that can enhance our physical health, improve digestion, and support mental clarity. By bringing awareness to our eating habits, engaging our senses, and making conscious choices, we can transform our relationship with food and cultivate a greater sense of well-being. Incorporate mindful eating into your daily life and observe the positive impact it has on your nourishment and clear thinking. Embrace this practice as a form of self-care and savor each moment of the eating experience, allowing yourself to fully enjoy and appreciate the nourishment it provides.

Chapter 23: Cultivating resilience to combat overthinking.

―――

I ntroduction:
Resilience is the ability to bounce back from adversity, navigate challenges, and adapt to change. When it comes to combating overthinking, developing resilience plays a crucial role in maintaining mental well-being and finding balance. In this chapter, we will explore strategies for cultivating resilience to overcome overthinking and build a more resilient mindset.

Understanding resilience:

Resilience is not an innate trait but rather a skill that can be developed and strengthened over time. It involves cultivating a positive mindset, managing stress effectively, and having the ability to adapt to new circumstances. By understanding the components of resilience, we can work towards enhancing our ability to cope with overthinking and life's challenges.

Building emotional resilience:

Emotional resilience is the capacity to manage and navigate our emotions in a healthy and constructive way. It involves developing self-awareness, practicing self-compassion, and building emotional intelligence. By cultivating emotional resilience, we can better regulate our emotions and prevent them from spiraling into overthinking patterns.

Developing a growth mindset:

A growth mindset is the belief that our abilities and intelligence can be developed through effort and learning. Embracing a growth mindset allows us to view challenges as opportunities for growth rather than obstacles to overcome. By shifting our perspective and embracing a growth mindset, we can approach overthinking with a sense of curiosity and a willingness to learn from our experiences.

Practicing self-compassion:

Self-compassion involves treating ourselves with kindness, understanding, and acceptance, particularly during times of struggle or self-doubt. When we experience overthinking, it is essential to cultivate self-compassion and offer ourselves the same support and understanding we would extend to a loved one. By practicing self-compassion, we can reduce self-criticism, cultivate resilience, and navigate overthinking with greater self-acceptance.

Developing problem-solving skills:

Resilience involves developing effective problem-solving skills to tackle challenges and find solutions. By enhancing our problem-solving abilities, we can approach overthinking from a proactive standpoint and work towards finding constructive solutions rather than getting stuck in a cycle of rumination. Developing problem-solving skills empowers us to take control of our thoughts and emotions, leading to greater mental clarity and resilience.

Cultivating social support:

Strong social connections and a supportive network are essential for resilience. Building and nurturing relationships with family, friends, or support groups can provide a sense of belonging and emotional support during challenging times. By cultivating social support, we have a network of people to turn to when overthinking becomes overwhelming, offering guidance, perspective, and encouragement.

Practicing mindfulness:

Mindfulness is a powerful tool for cultivating resilience and managing overthinking. By practicing mindfulness, we develop the ability to observe our thoughts and emotions without judgment, allowing us to detach from the constant rumination that often accompanies overthinking. Mindfulness also helps us stay grounded in the present moment, reducing anxiety and promoting mental clarity.

Setting realistic expectations:

Setting realistic expectations for ourselves and others is crucial for maintaining resilience and combating overthinking. Unrealistic expectations can lead to feelings of failure, self-doubt, and excessive worry. By setting attainable goals and understanding that perfection is not necessary, we can alleviate the pressure that often fuels overthinking and create a more resilient mindset.

Developing adaptive coping strategies:

Resilience involves developing adaptive coping strategies to manage stress and navigate challenging situations. Each person may have different strategies that work best for them, such as exercise, meditation, journaling, or seeking professional support. By exploring and incorporating adaptive coping strategies into our lives, we can better manage overthinking and build resilience in the face of adversity.

Learning from adversity:

Resilience is not about avoiding difficult situations but rather about learning from them and growing stronger as a result. When faced with challenges or setbacks, take the opportunity to reflect on the experience and identify any lessons that can be gained. Embrace adversity as a chance for personal growth and development, knowing that overcoming obstacles can lead to increased resilience and mental clarity.

Developing a supportive inner dialogue:

The way we talk to ourselves has a significant impact on our resilience and ability to combat overthinking. Cultivate a supportive inner dialogue that encourages self-belief, positive affirmations, and resilience-building statements. When faced with self-doubt or negative thoughts, challenge them with evidence of your past successes and strengths. By fostering a supportive inner dialogue, you can counteract the negative thought patterns that often accompany overthinking.

Cultivating flexibility:

Resilience involves being adaptable and flexible in the face of change and uncertainty. Life is filled with unexpected twists and turns, and cultivating flexibility allows us to navigate these challenges with greater ease. Embrace change as a natural part of life and develop the ability to adjust your plans and expectations when needed. By being flexible, you can reduce the impact of overthinking when faced with unexpected situations.

Seeking professional support:

Sometimes, overthinking can become overwhelming and challenging to manage on our own. In such cases, seeking professional support from a therapist or counselor can be immensely helpful. A mental health professional can provide guidance, coping strategies, and a safe space to explore and address underlying issues contributing to overthinking. Don't hesitate to reach out for support when needed; it is a sign of strength and resilience to ask for help.

Celebrating resilience:

Take the time to acknowledge and celebrate your resilience and progress in overcoming overthinking. Recognize the efforts you have made to cultivate resilience and the positive changes it has brought to your life. Celebrating resilience reinforces the belief in your ability to handle challenges and build mental clarity, motivating you to continue practicing resilience in the face of future obstacles.

Cultivating a sense of purpose:

Having a sense of purpose can provide direction and meaning to our lives, contributing to greater resilience and mental well-being. Reflect on your values, passions, and long-term goals to identify your sense of purpose. When faced with overthinking, remind yourself of your purpose and how it aligns with your actions and decisions. Cultivating a sense of purpose can provide a guiding light during challenging times, keeping you focused and motivated.

Building physical resilience:

Physical well-being is closely linked to mental resilience. Engage in regular exercise, prioritize adequate sleep, and maintain a balanced diet to support your overall health. Physical resilience can help you better cope with stress, reduce anxiety, and promote mental clarity. Make self-care a priority and notice how taking care of your body positively influences your ability to combat overthinking.

Practicing gratitude:

Cultivating a practice of gratitude can significantly contribute to resilience and mental clarity. Take time each day to reflect on the things you are grateful for, no matter how small they may seem. Gratitude shifts our focus from what is lacking to what we have, fostering a positive outlook and resilience in the face of challenges.

Embracing life's imperfections:

Resilience is not about being perfect or having all the answers. It's about accepting that life is filled with imperfections and uncertainties. Embrace the fact that overthinking and challenges are a natural part of the human experience. Let go of the need for everything to be perfect, and instead, focus on learning and growing from your experiences.

Conclusion:

Cultivating resilience is a powerful and transformative process that empowers us to combat overthinking and navigate life's challenges with greater clarity and strength. In this chapter, we have explored various strategies for cultivating resilience and building a more resilient mindset.

By understanding the components of resilience, such as emotional resilience, a growth mindset, self-compassion, problem-solving skills, and social support, we can lay a solid foundation for overcoming overthinking. Through practicing mindfulness, setting realistic expectations, and developing adaptive coping strategies, we can effectively manage stress and navigate difficult situations.

It is important to remember that resilience is not a destination but a continuous journey. It requires consistent effort, self-reflection, and a willingness to embrace change. As you continue to cultivate resilience, be patient and kind to yourself. Recognize that setbacks and challenges are opportunities for growth and learning.

Seeking professional support when needed is a sign of strength and a valuable resource in your resilience-building journey. Therapists and counselors can provide guidance, tools, and a supportive space to explore the underlying causes of overthinking and develop strategies for managing it effectively.

Celebrate your resilience along the way. Take pride in your progress and acknowledge the positive changes that resilience has brought to your life. By nurturing a sense of purpose, embracing life's imperfections, and practicing gratitude, you can further enhance your resilience and maintain a clear and focused mindset.

Remember, cultivating resilience is a lifelong practice. It will continue to support you in overcoming overthinking and facing future challenges with confidence and mental clarity. Embrace the journey, stay committed to your growth, and trust in your ability to break free from the overthinking trap.

In the next chapter, we will explore additional strategies for maintaining a clear and focused mindset, including techniques for stress relief and decluttering the mind. By incorporating these strategies into your daily life, you will continue to strengthen your resilience and experience greater peace and clarity.

Stay committed to your resilience-building journey and trust in your ability to overcome overthinking. You have the power to break free from its grip and live a life of clarity, purpose, and resilience.

Chapter 24: The power of breathwork for stress relief and mental clarity.

―――

I ntroduction:

In our fast-paced and demanding lives, stress has become a common companion. It can hinder our ability to think clearly, make decisions, and find inner peace. However, one of the most accessible and effective tools for managing stress and enhancing mental clarity is right at our fingertips: our breath. In this chapter, we will explore the power of breathwork as a tool for stress relief and cultivating mental clarity.

The connection between breath and stress:

Our breath is intimately connected to our emotions and physiological responses. When we are stressed or anxious, our breath tends to become shallow and rapid, fueling the stress response in our bodies. By consciously redirecting our breath, we can activate the relaxation response, reduce stress levels, and promote mental clarity.

Understanding breathwork:

Breathwork refers to a range of techniques and practices that involve conscious control and manipulation of the breath. These techniques have been utilized for centuries in various cultures and spiritual traditions to promote relaxation, healing, and self-awareness. Breathwork can involve deep diaphragmatic breathing, specific patterns of inhalation and exhalation, breath holds, and mindful awareness of the breath.

The benefits of breathwork:

Stress relief: Breathwork is an effective stress management tool. It activates the parasympathetic nervous system, which induces a state of relaxation, reduces stress hormones, and promotes a sense of calm and well-being.

Mental clarity: By focusing on the breath and regulating its rhythm, we can quiet the mind and enhance mental clarity. Breathwork brings us into the present moment, allowing us to let go of distracting thoughts and improve concentration and focus.

Emotional regulation: Breathwork can help regulate our emotions by calming the nervous system and creating a sense of balance. It can assist in releasing tension, anxiety, and overwhelm, allowing us to respond to challenging situations with greater emotional resilience and clarity.

Improved physical health: Deep, conscious breathing increases oxygenation in the body, promoting overall physical well-being. It can support cardiovascular health, boost the immune system, and aid in digestion.

Breathwork techniques for stress relief and mental clarity:

Diaphragmatic breathing: This technique involves breathing deeply into the belly, expanding the diaphragm. It promotes relaxation, activates the parasympathetic nervous system, and reduces stress.

Box breathing: In this technique, you inhale, hold the breath, exhale, and hold again, each for an equal count of time. It creates a balanced and steady rhythm, inducing a state of calm and mental clarity.

Alternate nostril breathing: This technique involves breathing through one nostril at a time while closing the other nostril. It balances the energy in the body, harmonizes the left and right hemispheres of the brain, and promotes mental balance.

4-7-8 breathing: This technique involves inhaling deeply through the nose for a count of 4, holding the breath for a count of 7, and exhaling slowly through the mouth for a count of 8. It promotes relaxation, reduces anxiety, and helps calm the mind.

Breath awareness meditation: This practice involves observing the natural flow of the breath without trying to control or change it. It cultivates mindfulness, presence, and a deep sense of calm.

Incorporating breathwork into daily life:

To reap the benefits of breathwork, it is essential to incorporate it into our daily routine. Here are some suggestions:

Morning routine: Start your day with a few minutes of intentional breathwork. It can help set a positive and calm tone for the day ahead.

Breath breaks: Take short breaks throughout the day to engage in a few minutes of focused breathwork. This can help reset your stress levels, clear your mind, and improve productivity.

Pre- and post-work rituals: Use breathwork techniques before and after work to transition into a focused and present mindset. It can help you release any work-related stress and enhance your ability to concentrate on the task at hand.

Stressful situations: When faced with challenging or stressful situations, take a moment to pause and engage in deep breathing. It can help calm your nervous system, reduce anxiety, and approach the situation with a clear and composed mind.

Bedtime routine: Incorporate breathwork into your bedtime routine to promote relaxation and prepare your mind and body for a restful sleep. It can help alleviate racing thoughts and promote a sense of tranquility.

Exploring breathwork practices:

There are various breathwork practices you can explore to deepen your experience and tailor it to your specific needs. Some practices include:

Pranayama: Pranayama is a yogic breathwork practice that involves specific techniques, such as Ujjayi breath, Kapalabhati, and Nadi Shodhana. These practices can have profound effects on calming the mind, balancing energy, and enhancing mental clarity.

Breathwork workshops and classes: Attend workshops or classes led by experienced breathwork facilitators. These sessions often incorporate specific breathwork techniques, guided meditation, and sound therapy to facilitate deep relaxation and mental clarity.

Breathwork apps and guided sessions: Explore breathwork apps and guided sessions available online. These resources provide structured guidance and offer a variety of breathwork techniques suitable for different needs and skill levels.

Conclusion:

Breathwork is a powerful tool for stress relief, mental clarity, and overall well-being. By consciously engaging with our breath and incorporating breathwork practices into our daily lives, we can tap into its transformative potential. Whether it's through deep diaphragmatic breathing, specific breathwork techniques, or breath awareness meditation, the power of breathwork can bring us back to the present moment, calm the mind, and cultivate mental clarity.

Experiment with different breathwork techniques, find what resonates with you, and create a consistent breathwork practice. As you embrace the power of breathwork, you will discover its ability to reduce overthinking, enhance focus, and promote a deep sense of calm and clarity in all aspects of your life.

In the next chapter, we will explore additional strategies for stress relief and mental clarity, including techniques for decluttering the mind and enhancing focus. These practices, combined with the power of breathwork, will further empower you to break free from overthinking and live a life of peace, presence, and mental well-being.

Chapter 25: Strategies for breaking free from overthinking triggers.

Introduction:

Overthinking can be triggered by various factors, such as stressful situations, negative emotions, perfectionism, or self-doubt. These triggers can lead to a cycle of rumination and excessive analysis that hinders our ability to find clarity and make sound decisions. In this chapter, we will explore effective strategies for identifying and breaking free from overthinking triggers.

Identifying overthinking triggers:

The first step in breaking free from overthinking triggers is to identify what sets off the overthinking cycle. Take some time to reflect on your patterns and notice the situations, emotions, or thoughts that tend to trigger overthinking. Common triggers may include:

Stressful events: Difficult work projects, relationship conflicts, or major life changes can trigger overthinking as we try to analyze and control the situation.

Negative emotions: Feelings of anxiety, fear, or self-doubt can fuel overthinking, as we try to find solutions or reassurance to alleviate these emotions.

Perfectionism: The pursuit of perfection can lead to overthinking as we excessively analyze our performance or strive for an ideal outcome.

External validation: Relying heavily on others' opinions or seeking constant reassurance can trigger overthinking as we try to anticipate their expectations and judgments.

Challenging limiting beliefs:

Overthinking is often fueled by limiting beliefs or irrational thought patterns. By challenging and reframing these beliefs, we can disrupt the overthinking cycle. Some strategies for challenging limiting beliefs include:

Questioning assumptions: Ask yourself if your beliefs are based on facts or assumptions. Are there alternative perspectives or possibilities that you haven't considered?

Gathering evidence: Look for evidence that contradicts your limiting beliefs. Focus on past successes or positive experiences that challenge the negative thoughts.

Rationalizing worst-case scenarios: Analyze the likelihood and impact of the worst-case scenarios you fear. Often, we catastrophize situations, and examining them rationally can help us gain perspective.

Practicing self-compassion: Replace self-critical thoughts with self-compassionate and realistic statements. Treat yourself with kindness and understanding, acknowledging that nobody is perfect.

Building resilience:

Developing resilience can help break free from overthinking triggers and navigate challenges with greater ease. Resilience-building strategies include:

Cultivating self-care: Prioritize self-care activities that nurture your physical, mental, and emotional well-being. Engage in activities that replenish your energy and reduce stress.

Developing coping skills: Explore healthy coping mechanisms such as exercise, mindfulness, journaling, or talking to a supportive friend. These practices can help you manage stress and negative emotions effectively.

Setting boundaries: Establish clear boundaries in your personal and professional life to protect your time, energy, and mental well-being. Say no when necessary and create space for self-reflection and rejuvenation.

Embracing change and uncertainty: Practice adaptability and acceptance of the inevitable changes and uncertainties of life. Develop a growth mindset that sees challenges as opportunities for growth and learning.

Engaging in mindful awareness:

Mindful awareness can help break free from overthinking triggers by grounding us in the present moment and reducing the power of intrusive thoughts. Try the following techniques:

Mindful breathing: Focus on your breath, observing each inhalation and exhalation without judgment. This anchors your attention to the present and calms the mind.

Body scan meditation: Scan your body from head to toe, paying attention to any sensations or areas of tension. This helps you reconnect with your physical body and release mental tension.

Noticing thoughts: Practice observing your thoughts without getting caught up in them or reacting to them. Simply acknowledge them as passing mental events and let them go without judgment.

Sensory awareness: Engage your senses fully in the present moment. Notice the sights, sounds, smells, tastes, and textures around you. This helps shift your focus away from overthinking and into the present experience.

Developing action plans:

Once you have identified your overthinking triggers and explored strategies for breaking free from them, it's important to develop action plans to implement these strategies effectively. Consider the following steps:

Awareness: Be mindful of your triggers and recognize when you're starting to engage in overthinking. This self-awareness is crucial for initiating the action plan.

Intervention techniques: Implement the strategies you've learned to disrupt the overthinking cycle. This may involve challenging limiting beliefs, practicing mindfulness, engaging in self-care, or seeking support from others.

Coping mechanisms: Identify healthy coping mechanisms that work best for you in managing stress and redirecting your focus away from overthinking triggers. This could include physical exercise, creative outlets, relaxation techniques, or engaging in hobbies.

Support system: Reach out to trusted friends, family members, or professionals who can provide guidance and support as you navigate your overthinking triggers. Share your struggles and progress with them, and lean on them when needed.

Reflection and adaptation:

Regularly reflect on your progress and make any necessary adaptations to your action plan. Overcoming overthinking is a journey, and what works for one person may not work for another. Be open to trying new strategies, modifying existing ones, and finding what works best for you.

Conclusion:

Breaking free from overthinking triggers requires self-awareness, resilience, and the willingness to challenge limiting beliefs. By implementing the strategies outlined in this chapter, you can gain control over your overthinking tendencies and cultivate mental clarity.

Remember, overcoming overthinking is a gradual process that requires patience and persistence. Celebrate your small victories along the way and be compassionate with yourself during setbacks. With time and practice, you can develop the skills to navigate life's challenges with a clear and focused mind.

In the next chapter, we will delve into effective techniques for decluttering the mind, organizing thoughts, and enhancing focus. These practices will further support you in your journey to break free from overthinking and live a more present and fulfilling life.

Chapter 26: Balancing information intake in the digital age.

———

I ntroduction:

In today's digital age, we have access to an overwhelming amount of information at our fingertips. While this has its benefits, such as instant connectivity and vast knowledge resources, it also poses challenges in terms of information overload and the potential for excessive consumption. In this chapter, we will explore strategies for balancing information intake in the digital age to maintain mental clarity and prevent the negative effects of information overwhelm.

Understanding information overload:

Information overload occurs when we are exposed to more information than we can effectively process or utilize. It can lead to cognitive overload, decreased productivity, and increased stress levels. Recognizing the signs of information overload is the first step in finding balance. Common symptoms include:

1.Difficulty focusing or making decisions due to an overwhelming amount of information.

2.Feeling constantly distracted by notifications, emails, and social media updates.

3.Increased anxiety or stress levels caused by the pressure to keep up with an ever-growing stream of information.

4. Reduced ability to retain information or engage in deep, meaningful thinking due to constant information consumption.

Intentional information consumption:

To find balance in the digital age, it is important to adopt intentional information consumption habits. Consider the following strategies:

Define your purpose: Clarify why you are seeking information and what you hope to gain from it. This will help you filter out irrelevant or unnecessary information and focus on what truly matters to you.

Curate your sources: Choose reputable and reliable sources of information that align with your interests and goals. Be selective in the platforms and channels you follow to avoid being overwhelmed by a barrage of information.

Set boundaries: Establish boundaries for your information consumption. Determine specific times or durations for checking emails, browsing social media, or reading news articles. Avoid mindless scrolling or falling into the trap of continuous information consumption.

Practice digital detoxes: Take regular breaks from digital devices and platforms. Designate tech-free periods or days to recharge, engage in offline activities, and allow your mind to rest from the constant influx of information.

Develop critical thinking skills:

In the face of abundant information, developing strong critical thinking skills becomes crucial. This allows you to evaluate and analyze information effectively. Consider the following approaches:

Verify sources: Cross-reference information from multiple reliable sources to ensure accuracy and avoid falling prey to misinformation or fake news.

Evaluate credibility: Assess the credibility of the sources you encounter. Consider factors such as expertise, reputation, and objectivity before accepting information as valid.

Analyze bias: Be aware of potential biases in the information you consume. Recognize that various sources may present information from different perspectives, and strive to seek a balanced understanding.

Practice skepticism: Question assumptions and claims presented in the information you come across. Look for supporting evidence and logical reasoning before accepting or sharing information.

Digital well-being practices:

To maintain mental clarity and prevent information overload, incorporate digital well-being practices into your routine. These practices include:

Mindful information consumption: Practice mindfulness while engaging with digital content. Be fully present and conscious of your intention when consuming information, avoiding mindless scrolling or jumping from one topic to another without purpose.

Regular information Cleanse: Periodically declutter your digital life by unsubscribing from unnecessary newsletters, unfollowing irrelevant accounts, and organizing your digital files. This reduces digital noise and helps you focus on what truly matters.

Engage in offline activities: Dedicate time to engage in offline activities that nurture your well-being and allow you to disconnect from the digital world. This could include hobbies, exercise, spending time in nature, or quality face-to-face interactions.

Prioritize deep work:

Prioritize deep work: Deep work refers to the ability to focus without distraction on cognitively demanding tasks. Create dedicated blocks of time during your day where you can engage in deep work without interruptions from digital devices or information sources. This allows you to fully immerse yourself in meaningful and productive work, free from the constant distractions of the digital world.

Practice digital mindfulness: Incorporate mindfulness techniques into your digital activities. Before engaging with digital content, take a moment to check in with yourself and assess your mental state. Set clear intentions for your online activities and be mindful of how they affect your well-being.

Practice digital sabbaticals: Take extended periods of time away from digital devices and information consumption. This could be a weekend retreat, a vacation, or even a technology-free day each week. Use this time to recharge, reconnect with yourself and others, and gain perspective on your relationship with information.

Engaging in critical information evaluation:

In a digital world filled with information, it is essential to develop the skills to critically evaluate the information we encounter. Consider the following practices:

Fact-checking: Verify the accuracy of the information you come across by fact-checking with reliable sources. Look for corroborating evidence and cross-reference information before accepting it as true.

Questioning assumptions: Challenge your own assumptions and biases when evaluating information. Be open to considering different perspectives and weigh the evidence objectively.

Discerning reliable sources: Learn to identify reputable and trustworthy sources of information. Consider the expertise, credibility, and objectivity of the sources you rely on.

Understanding context: Contextualize the information you consume by considering the larger picture. Understand the background, circumstances, and motivations behind the information to gain a more nuanced understanding.

Maintaining emotional well-being:

Excessive information consumption can have a negative impact on emotional well-being. To maintain balance, consider the following practices:

Emotional awareness: Be mindful of how the information you consume affects your emotions. Notice any feelings of overwhelm, anxiety, or stress, and take steps to address them, such as practicing self-care or seeking support.

Setting emotional boundaries: Set boundaries around the types of information that trigger negative emotions or disrupt your well-being. Limit exposure to content that is distressing or causes unnecessary emotional turmoil.

Practicing self-compassion: Be kind to yourself when navigating the vast amount of information available. Recognize that you cannot consume everything, and it's okay to prioritize your well-being over constant information intake.

Conclusion:

Balancing information intake in the digital age is essential for maintaining mental clarity, emotional well-being, and overall life balance. By developing intentional information consumption habits, honing critical thinking skills, and prioritizing digital well-being practices, you can navigate the information landscape effectively and prevent the negative effects of information overload. Remember to approach information with mindfulness, discernment, and self-care, ensuring that you remain in control of the information you consume rather than letting it consume you.

In the next chapter, we will explore strategies for cultivating focus and concentration in an age of distractions. These techniques will further support you in maintaining mental clarity and productivity amidst the digital noise.

Chapter 27: Overcoming self-doubt and building self-confidence.

———

I ntroduction:

Self-doubt can be a significant obstacle on the path to personal growth and success. It can hinder our ability to take risks, pursue our goals, and fully realize our potential. In this chapter, we will explore strategies for overcoming self-doubt and building self-confidence. By understanding the root causes of self-doubt and implementing effective techniques, you can develop a strong belief in yourself and your abilities.

Understanding self-doubt:

Self-doubt is the lack of confidence or belief in oneself. It can stem from various sources, such as past failures, negative self-talk, comparison to others, or fear of judgment. Recognizing the signs of self-doubt is crucial in order to address and overcome it. Common symptoms include:

1. Persistent negative self-talk, focusing on weaknesses or past mistakes.

2. Feeling inadequate or unworthy of success.

3. Avoidance of new challenges or opportunities due to fear of failure or rejection.

4. Constantly seeking validation from others to boost self-esteem.

Challenging negative self-talk:

Negative self-talk is a primary contributor to self-doubt. To overcome self-doubt, it is essential to challenge and reframe negative self-talk. Consider the following strategies:

Awareness: Pay attention to your inner dialogue and become aware of negative self-talk patterns. Recognize when you are being self-critical or overly harsh in your self-assessment.

Questioning: Challenge the validity of negative thoughts by questioning their accuracy and evidence. Ask yourself if there is any real basis for the negative beliefs you hold about yourself.

Reframing: Replace negative self-talk with positive and empowering statements. Affirm your strengths, accomplishments, and potential. Practice self-compassion and kindness towards yourself.

Visualization: Use visualization techniques to imagine yourself succeeding and overcoming challenges. Create vivid mental images of yourself confident and capable, achieving your goals and dreams.

Cultivating self-compassion:

Self-compassion is a powerful tool for building self-confidence and overcoming self-doubt. It involves treating yourself with kindness, understanding, and acceptance, particularly in the face of failure or setbacks. Consider the following practices:

Self-acceptance: Embrace your imperfections and acknowledge that everyone makes mistakes. Understand that failure is a natural part of the learning process and does not define your worth.

Mindful self-compassion: Practice being present and non-judgmental towards yourself. Instead of beating yourself up over mistakes, offer yourself kindness and understanding.

Self-care: Prioritize self-care activities that nurture your physical, emotional, and mental well-being. Engage in activities that bring you joy, relaxation, and rejuvenation.

Supportive inner dialogue: Develop a supportive and encouraging inner voice. Replace self-criticism with words of encouragement and affirmation. Treat yourself as you would a close friend or loved one.

Setting achievable goals:

Setting achievable goals is crucial for building self-confidence. When we set realistic goals and take steps towards achieving them, we prove to ourselves that we are capable and competent. Consider the following strategies:

Break it down: Break larger goals into smaller, manageable steps. This allows for a sense of progress and accomplishment along the way.

Celebrate milestones: Acknowledge and celebrate your achievements, no matter how small. Recognize your progress and use it as motivation to continue moving forward.

Embrace growth mindset: Adopt a growth mindset, understanding that abilities and skills can be developed through effort and practice. Embrace challenges as opportunities for growth and learning.

Reflect on past successes and strengths: Reflect on past successes and times when you have overcome challenges or achieved your goals. Remind yourself of your capabilities and strengths. Use these positive experiences as evidence that you are capable of overcoming self-doubt and achieving your aspirations.

Surrounding yourself with support:

Surrounding yourself with a supportive network can significantly impact your self-confidence. Seek out individuals who believe in you, encourage your growth, and provide constructive feedback. Consider the following:

Supportive relationships: Build relationships with people who uplift and inspire you. Surround yourself with individuals who have confidence in your abilities and support your goals.

Accountability partners: Find an accountability partner or join a support group where you can share your challenges and progress. Having someone to hold you accountable and offer guidance can boost your confidence.

Seek mentorship: Find mentors or role models who have overcome self-doubt and achieved success in areas that resonate with you. Learn from their experiences and seek guidance and advice.

Embracing failure as a learning opportunity:

Fear of failure often fuels self-doubt. However, failure is a natural part of the growth process and provides valuable learning opportunities. Consider the following mindset shifts:

Reframe failure: Instead of viewing failure as a reflection of your worth or abilities, reframe it as a stepping stone toward success. Embrace failure as an opportunity to learn, grow, and improve.

Learn from setbacks: Analyze your failures or setbacks objectively. Identify what went wrong and the lessons you can take from the experience. Use this knowledge to adjust your approach and make informed decisions.

Embrace a growth mindset: Embrace a growth mindset, understanding that setbacks and challenges are part of the journey. Believe in your ability to learn and improve through perseverance and effort.

Stepping outside your comfort zone:

Stepping outside your comfort zone is essential for building self-confidence and overcoming self-doubt. By taking risks and facing challenges, you expand your comfort zone and prove to yourself that you are capable of more than you think. Consider the following:

Start small: Begin by taking small steps outside your comfort zone. Gradually increase the level of difficulty as you become more comfortable with discomfort.

Embrace challenges: Embrace opportunities that stretch your abilities and push you beyond your familiar limits. Embracing challenges allows you to discover your untapped potential and build self-confidence.

Focus on progress, not perfection: Shift your focus from perfection to progress. Celebrate the effort and growth you make, rather than aiming for flawless outcomes.

Conclusion:

Overcoming self-doubt and building self-confidence is a journey that requires self-awareness, resilience, and deliberate action. By challenging negative self-talk, cultivating self-compassion, setting achievable goals, seeking support, embracing failure as a learning opportunity, and stepping outside your comfort zone, you can develop a strong sense of self-confidence and overcome self-doubt. Remember, self-confidence is not about being flawless or never experiencing self-doubt; it is about recognizing your worth, believing in your abilities, and persevering through challenges with resilience and determination. In the next chapter, we will explore strategies for maintaining motivation and staying focused on your goals.

Chapter 28: Practicing forgiveness and letting go of regret.

———

I ntroduction:

Regret and holding onto grudges can weigh us down and hinder our personal growth. In this chapter, we will explore the importance of practicing forgiveness and letting go of regret. By understanding the impact of these emotions on our well-being and implementing effective strategies, we can free ourselves from the burden of the past and create a more fulfilling present and future.

Understanding regret:

Regret is a feeling of sadness, disappointment, or remorse over past actions, choices, or missed opportunities. It can lead to negative emotions such as guilt, shame, and self-blame. Recognizing the presence of regret in our lives is the first step towards addressing it and finding healing.

Reflecting on past actions: Take time to reflect on the actions, decisions, or situations that have caused you regret. Understand the underlying reasons for these regrets and the impact they have had on your life.

Acknowledging emotions: Allow yourself to fully feel the emotions associated with regret. It's important to acknowledge and validate your feelings in order to move forward.

Learning from mistakes: Use regret as an opportunity for growth and learning. Identify the lessons you have learned from your past experiences and apply them to your present and future choices.

The power of forgiveness:

Forgiveness is a transformative act that liberates us from the grip of resentment and anger. It is not about condoning or forgetting past wrongs but rather about freeing ourselves from the emotional burden they carry. Consider the following aspects of forgiveness:

Letting go of resentment: Forgiveness allows us to release the resentment we hold towards others who have wronged us. By forgiving, we choose to free ourselves from the negative emotions associated with the past.

Self-forgiveness: Equally important is the practice of self-forgiveness. We all make mistakes, and holding onto self-blame and guilt can be detrimental to our well-being. By forgiving ourselves, we allow room for self-compassion and growth.

Healing relationships: Forgiveness can also contribute to healing and restoring relationships. It opens the door to reconciliation and the possibility of rebuilding trust and understanding.

Unburdening yourself: Forgiveness is a way to unburden yourself from carrying the weight of past grievances. It liberates your energy and allows you to focus on the present and future rather than being consumed by the past.

The process of forgiveness:

Practicing forgiveness is a process that requires time, effort, and self-reflection. Consider the following steps to cultivate forgiveness:

Reflect and accept: Reflect on the past events or actions that have caused you pain or regret. Accept the reality of what has happened and the emotions associated with it.

Empathy and compassion: Seek to understand the perspective of those who have wronged you. Practice empathy and compassion, recognizing that everyone has their own struggles and flaws.

Release and let go: Choose to release the negative emotions and resentment associated with the past. This may involve writing a forgiveness letter, engaging in a forgiveness ritual, or simply making a conscious decision to let go.

Practice self-compassion: Extend forgiveness to yourself. Recognize that you are human, capable of making mistakes, and deserving of self-compassion and understanding.

Cultivating a present-centered mindset:

Letting go of regret involves shifting our focus from the past to the present. By cultivating a present-centered mindset, we can fully engage in the here and now, creating a more fulfilling and purposeful life. Consider the following practices:

Mindfulness: Practice mindfulness to cultivate awareness of the present moment. By focusing on the here and now, you can let go of regrets and embrace the opportunities that lie ahead.

Gratitude: Cultivate a sense of gratitude for what you have in the present moment. Appreciate the blessings and positive aspects of your life, shifting your focus from past regrets to present abundance.

Self-reflection: Engage in regular self-reflection to gain clarity on your values, goals, and aspirations. This allows you to align your actions with your authentic self and make choices that align with your true desires.

Self-care: Prioritize self-care practices that nourish your mind, body, and soul. Taking care of yourself physically, emotionally, and mentally enables you to let go of regrets and focus on personal growth and well-being.

Moving forward with purpose:

Once you have practiced forgiveness and let go of regret, it's important to move forward with purpose. Consider the following strategies:

Setting meaningful goals: Define goals that align with your values and aspirations. Having clear objectives and a sense of purpose can motivate you to take positive action and create a fulfilling future.

Learning from the past: Use the lessons learned from past regrets to make informed decisions in the present. Apply the wisdom gained from your experiences to navigate future challenges and avoid repeating past mistakes.

Embracing growth mindset: Adopt a growth mindset that sees failures and setbacks as opportunities for learning and growth. Embrace challenges and view them as stepping stones on your journey towards personal and professional development.

Seeking support: Surround yourself with a supportive network of friends, family, or mentors who can provide guidance, encouragement, and accountability as you move forward. Share your aspirations and challenges with trusted individuals who can offer valuable insights and support.

Conclusion:

Practicing forgiveness and letting go of regret is a powerful process that allows us to release the burdens of the past and create a more fulfilling present and future. By understanding the impact of regret, embracing forgiveness, cultivating a present-centered mindset, and moving forward with purpose, we can free ourselves from the shackles of the past and embark on a journey of growth and self-discovery. Remember, it is never too late to let go of regrets and create a life that is filled with joy, purpose, and fulfillment. In the next chapter, we will explore strategies for embracing change and navigating transitions in life.

Chapter 29: The role of sleep and rest in mental clarity.

———

Introduction:

In today's fast-paced and demanding world, finding moments of rest and rejuvenation is crucial for maintaining mental clarity and overall well-being. In this chapter, we will explore the importance of sleep and rest in promoting mental clarity and offer practical strategies for optimizing your sleep and incorporating restful practices into your daily life.

Understanding the importance of sleep:

Sleep is a fundamental biological process that plays a vital role in promoting mental clarity, cognitive function, and emotional well-being. Consider the following aspects of sleep:

Restorative nature: During sleep, the body undergoes essential processes such as tissue repair, hormone regulation, and memory consolidation. Getting sufficient sleep allows the brain to recharge and rejuvenate, leading to improved mental clarity and cognitive performance.

Emotional regulation: Sleep plays a significant role in regulating emotions and managing stress. Lack of sleep can lead to increased irritability, mood swings, and difficulty in regulating emotions, which can negatively impact mental clarity and overall mental health.

Brain health and memory: Adequate sleep is crucial for optimal brain function and memory consolidation. During sleep, the brain processes and organizes information, strengthening neural connections and enhancing learning and memory retention.

Establishing healthy sleep habits:

To optimize sleep and promote mental clarity, it's important to establish healthy sleep habits. Consider the following strategies:

Consistent sleep schedule: Set a regular sleep schedule by going to bed and waking up at the same time each day, even on weekends. This helps regulate your body's internal clock and promotes better sleep quality.

Creating a sleep-friendly environment: Design your bedroom to be conducive to sleep. Ensure a comfortable mattress and pillow, minimize noise and light disruptions, and maintain a cool, dark, and quiet environment that promotes relaxation.

Bedtime routine: Establish a relaxing bedtime routine to signal to your body that it's time to wind down. Engage in activities such as reading, taking a warm bath, or practicing relaxation techniques like deep breathing or meditation.

Limiting stimulants and electronics: Avoid consuming caffeine, nicotine, or alcohol close to bedtime as they can interfere with sleep quality. Additionally, limit the use of electronic devices before bed as the blue light emitted from screens can disrupt your natural sleep-wake cycle.

Incorporating restful practices:

In addition to getting sufficient sleep, incorporating restful practices throughout the day can further enhance mental clarity. Consider the following strategies:

Taking regular breaks: Incorporate short breaks into your daily routine to rest and recharge. Engage in activities that help you relax and reset, such as stretching, going for a walk, or practicing mindfulness.

Mindful rest: Practice mindful rest by intentionally engaging in activities that bring you joy and relaxation. This could include hobbies, spending time in nature, listening to music, or practicing gentle yoga or meditation.

Power napping: If you feel fatigued during the day, consider taking a short power nap of around 20-30 minutes. Power naps can boost alertness, productivity, and mental clarity, but be mindful not to nap too close to bedtime to avoid disrupting nighttime sleep.

Balancing activity and rest: Strive for a balance between activity and rest in your daily life. Recognize when you need to pause and recharge, allowing yourself moments of rest to prevent burnout and maintain mental clarity.

Prioritizing self-care:

Self-care is a crucial component of promoting mental clarity and well-being. It involves nurturing your physical, emotional, and mental health through intentional practices. Consider the following self-care strategies:

Healthy lifestyle choices: Adopt a balanced diet, engage in regular physical exercise, and manage stress through techniques like meditation or deep breathing. These practices support overall well-being and contribute to better sleep quality and mental clarity.

Stress management: Find effective ways to manage stress in your life. This may include practicing stress-reducing techniques such as mindfulness, journaling, or engaging in hobbies and activities that bring you joy and relaxation. By managing stress, you can create a more peaceful and restful state of mind, which in turn supports better sleep and mental clarity.

Emotional well-being: Pay attention to your emotional well-being and take steps to nurture it. This may involve seeking support from loved ones or a therapist, practicing self-compassion and self-acceptance, and engaging in activities that promote emotional balance and fulfillment.

Relaxation techniques: Incorporate relaxation techniques into your daily routine to promote restful sleep and mental clarity. These may include progressive muscle relaxation, guided imagery, aromatherapy, or listening to calming music. Experiment with different techniques to find what works best for you.

Conclusion:

Sleep and rest are essential components of maintaining mental clarity and overall well-being. By prioritizing sleep, establishing healthy sleep habits, and incorporating restful practices into your daily life, you can optimize your cognitive function, emotional well-being, and overall mental clarity.

Remember that everyone's sleep needs and restful practices may differ, so it's important to listen to your body and find what works best for you. Experiment with different strategies and techniques, and be patient with yourself as you cultivate habits that promote restful sleep and mental clarity.

In the next chapter, we will explore the power of gratitude and its impact on mental well-being.

Chapter 30: Techniques for redirecting overthinking energy into productivity.

———

I ntroduction:

Overthinking can consume our mental energy and hinder our productivity. However, with the right strategies, we can learn to redirect that overthinking energy towards more productive pursuits. In this chapter, we will explore techniques and strategies that can help you harness the power of overthinking and channel it into productive endeavors.

Recognizing overthinking patterns:

The first step in redirecting overthinking energy is to become aware of your overthinking patterns. Pay attention to the situations or triggers that lead to overthinking. Are there specific topics, uncertainties, or challenges that tend to occupy your mind excessively? By identifying these patterns, you can begin to address them more effectively.

Reframing overthinking as problem-solving:

Instead of viewing overthinking as a negative habit, reframe it as an opportunity for problem-solving. When you catch yourself overthinking, ask yourself if there is a specific problem or challenge that needs your attention. By shifting your perspective, you can direct your energy towards finding solutions and taking productive action.

Setting clear goals and priorities:

Setting clear goals and priorities can help you focus your energy on tasks that matter most. Take some time to define your short-term and long-term goals and break them down into actionable steps. By having a clear roadmap, you can channel your overthinking energy into planning and taking purposeful actions towards achieving your objectives.

Creating action plans:

Once you have established your goals, create action plans to guide your progress. Break down your goals into smaller, manageable tasks, and create a schedule or to-do list. This will provide you with a structured framework to follow, reducing the chances of getting caught up in overthinking and increasing your productivity.

Practicing time blocking:

Time blocking is a technique that involves allocating specific time slots for different activities or tasks. By scheduling dedicated blocks of time for specific tasks or projects, you create a sense of structure and focus. This helps to minimize distractions and prevents overthinking from taking over. Set aside time for focused work, breaks, and relaxation to maintain a healthy balance.

Embracing mindfulness:

Mindfulness can be a powerful tool for redirecting overthinking energy. Practice being fully present in the current moment, observing your thoughts without judgment. This cultivates awareness and helps you detach from excessive rumination. Engage in mindfulness exercises such as meditation, deep breathing, or body scans to calm the mind and increase your ability to focus on productive tasks.

Utilizing visualization techniques:

Visualization techniques involve creating mental images of successfully completing tasks or achieving desired outcomes. Visualize yourself engaging in productive activities, staying focused, and accomplishing your goals. This technique helps to rewire your brain, making it easier to shift from overthinking to productive action.

Implementing pomodoro technique:

The Pomodoro Technique is a time-management method that involves working in focused intervals, typically 25 minutes, followed by short breaks. This structured approach can help you break down tasks into manageable chunks and maintain focus. By giving yourself designated breaks, you can recharge and prevent mental fatigue, which can contribute to overthinking.

Practicing active problem-solving:

If you find yourself overthinking a particular problem or challenge, engage in active problem-solving techniques. Write down the issue at hand, brainstorm potential solutions, and evaluate their pros and cons. Taking proactive steps towards finding solutions will redirect your overthinking energy into productive problem-solving.

Engaging in physical activity:

Physical activity is not only beneficial for your overall well-being but also for redirecting overthinking energy. Engage in regular exercise or physical activities that you enjoy. Physical movement releases endorphins, reduces stress, and enhances focus, making it easier to channel your overthinking energy into productive endeavors. Whether it's going for a jog, practicing yoga, or engaging in a team sport, physical activity can help clear your mind, increase your energy levels, and improve your overall cognitive function.

Using external tools and resources:

There are various tools and resources available that can assist you in redirecting overthinking energy into productivity. For example, productivity apps and software can help you organize tasks, set reminders, and track your progress. Time management techniques, such as the Eisenhower Matrix or the Kanban method, can provide structure and clarity in prioritizing tasks.

Seeking accountability:

Accountability can be a powerful motivator for redirecting overthinking energy. Find an accountability partner or join a group or community that shares similar goals or interests. By regularly checking in with someone or sharing your progress and challenges, you can stay focused, maintain momentum, and overcome the tendency to overthink.

Embracing imperfect action:

Overthinking often stems from a fear of making mistakes or not meeting expectations. Embrace the concept of imperfect action and give yourself permission to make mistakes along the way. Remember that taking action, even if it's not perfect, is better than endlessly ruminating and not moving forward. Learn from your mistakes and use them as opportunities for growth and improvement.

Celebrating small wins:

Recognize and celebrate your achievements, no matter how small they may seem. Acknowledging your progress and giving yourself credit for the tasks you've completed can boost your motivation and self-confidence. This positive reinforcement will help you stay motivated, maintain momentum, and shift your focus from overthinking to recognizing your accomplishments.

Practicing self-care:

Self-care plays a crucial role in redirecting overthinking energy into productivity. Take care of your physical, mental, and emotional well-being by getting enough rest, nourishing your body with healthy food, and engaging in activities that bring you joy and relaxation. When you prioritize self-care, you create a foundation of well-being that supports productive thinking and action.

Limiting distractions:

Identify and minimize distractions that contribute to overthinking. This may involve turning off notifications on your phone, creating a dedicated workspace, or setting boundaries with colleagues or family members. By creating an environment that is conducive to focused work, you can minimize distractions and maximize your productivity.

Practicing effective decision-making:

Overthinking often arises when faced with decisions, big or small. Develop effective decision-making skills by gathering relevant information, weighing the pros and cons, and trusting your intuition. Avoid getting caught up in analysis paralysis by setting deadlines for decision-making and being willing to make adjustments if needed.

Reflecting and learning from experience:

Take time to reflect on your experiences and learn from them. Review past situations where overthinking may have hindered your productivity and identify strategies that helped you redirect your energy effectively. By understanding your own patterns and learning from past experiences, you can develop a toolkit of techniques that work best for you.

Conclusion:

Redirecting overthinking energy into productivity is a skill that can be developed with practice and self-awareness. By implementing these techniques, you can harness the power of overthinking and channel it into productive endeavors. Remember to be patient with yourself, celebrate your progress, and adapt these strategies to suit your individual needs and preferences.

In the next chapter, we will explore techniques for maintaining a balanced lifestyle to support long-term mental clarity and productivity.

Chapter 31: Cultivating mindful habits for sustained mental clarity.

———

I ntroduction:

In our fast-paced and constantly connected world, it's easy to get caught up in the chaos and lose sight of mental clarity. However, by cultivating mindful habits, we can create a solid foundation for sustained mental clarity and well-being. In this chapter, we will explore various practices and techniques that can help us develop mindful habits and enhance our ability to stay present, focused, and clear-headed.

Morning rituals:

Start your day with intention by incorporating mindful practices into your morning routine. This could include activities such as meditation, journaling, stretching, or simply taking a few moments to set positive intentions for the day ahead. By creating a peaceful and reflective space in the morning, you set the tone for a day filled with mental clarity and mindfulness.

Mindful eating:

Pay attention to what and how you eat. Engage all your senses during meals, savoring each bite and appreciating the nourishment that food provides. Avoid multitasking while eating, and instead, focus solely on the experience of nourishing your body. By practicing mindful eating, you can enhance your digestion, increase your enjoyment of food, and promote mental clarity.

Breath awareness:

Throughout the day, take moments to pause and bring your attention to your breath. Notice the sensation of the breath entering and leaving your body, and use it as an anchor to bring yourself back to the present moment. Deep, conscious breathing can help calm the mind, reduce stress, and increase mental clarity.

Digital detox:

In an era of constant digital stimulation, it's essential to take regular breaks from screens and technology. Set aside specific times each day to disconnect from your devices and engage in activities that promote mindfulness, such as going for a walk in nature, reading a book, or engaging in creative pursuits. By giving yourself space from constant digital input, you can cultivate mental clarity and reduce distractions.

Mindful movement:

Incorporate mindful movement practices into your daily routine, such as yoga, tai chi, or qigong. These practices encourage a mind-body connection, promote relaxation, and improve focus. By moving with intention and awareness, you can cultivate mental clarity and reduce the impact of stress on your mind and body.

Gratitude practice:

Develop a gratitude practice to cultivate a positive mindset and enhance mental clarity. Take time each day to reflect on the things you are grateful for, whether big or small. This practice can shift your focus from negative thinking to a more positive and appreciative mindset, allowing for greater clarity and a sense of well-being.

Mindful communication:

Pay attention to your words and how you communicate with others. Practice active listening, being fully present in conversations, and speaking with kindness and compassion. By cultivating mindful communication, you can enhance your connections with others, reduce misunderstandings, and promote clear and effective communication.

Regular mindfulness meditation:

Make mindfulness meditation a regular practice in your life. Set aside dedicated time each day to sit in stillness and observe your thoughts and sensations without judgment. Mindfulness meditation trains the mind to be present and focused, allowing for greater mental clarity and the ability to let go of overthinking and distractions.

Mindful breaks:

Incorporate short mindful breaks throughout your day. Take a few moments to step away from your work or tasks, close your eyes, and bring your attention to your breath or the present moment. These short breaks can help refresh your mind, reduce stress, and improve overall mental clarity.

Evening reflection:

End your day with a period of reflection and gratitude. Take a few moments to review the events of the day, acknowledging both the challenges and the positive moments. Practice gratitude for the lessons learned and the opportunities for growth. This evening reflection can help you gain perspective, let go of any lingering overthinking, and prepare for a restful and rejuvenating sleep.

Mindful technology use:

Be intentional and mindful in your use of technology. Set boundaries and limits for screen time, prioritize meaningful interactions over mindless scrolling, and be aware of how certain digital activities may affect your mental clarity. Use technology as a tool for connection, learning, and inspiration, rather than as a source of distraction or overwhelm.

Mindful breathing breaks:

Throughout the day, take intentional breathing breaks to recenter and ground yourself. Close your eyes, take a deep breath in, and exhale fully, focusing on the sensation of the breath entering and leaving your body. This simple practice can help you release tension, clear your mind, and return to the present moment with renewed clarity.

Mindful work practices:

Incorporate mindfulness into your work routine. Before diving into tasks, take a moment to set clear intentions and prioritize your activities. Practice single-tasking, focusing on one task at a time, and give it your full attention. Take short breaks between tasks to stretch, breathe, or simply rest your mind. By bringing mindfulness into your work practices, you can enhance productivity, reduce stress, and maintain mental clarity.

Mindful body scan:

Engage in a mindful body scan practice to connect with your physical sensations and release tension. Close your eyes and systematically bring your attention to each part of your body, starting from your toes and moving up to the top of your head. Notice any areas of tension or discomfort, and allow them to soften and release as you breathe deeply. This practice promotes relaxation, body awareness, and mental clarity.

Mindful leisure activities:

When engaging in leisure activities, such as hobbies, sports, or creative pursuits, bring a sense of mindfulness to the experience. Be fully present, savoring each moment and immersing yourself in the activity. Whether it's painting, playing a musical instrument, or engaging in a physical workout, practicing mindfulness can enhance your enjoyment, focus, and mental clarity.

Mindful self-reflection:

Take regular moments for self-reflection and introspection. Set aside dedicated time to check in with yourself, assess your thoughts and emotions, and gain insight into your patterns and behaviors. This practice of self-reflection can provide valuable clarity and help you make conscious choices aligned with your values and goals.

Mindful environmental awareness:

Pay attention to your surroundings and develop a sense of environmental awareness. Notice the sights, sounds, smells, and textures around you. Practice gratitude for the beauty of nature and the simple joys of everyday life. By cultivating a sense of connection with your environment, you can enhance your overall well-being and mental clarity.

Mindful stress management:

When faced with stress or challenges, approach them with mindfulness. Instead of reacting impulsively or becoming overwhelmed, pause and take a few deep breaths. Acknowledge your emotions and thoughts without judgment, and then choose a response that aligns with your values and promotes mental clarity. Mindful stress management techniques, such as progressive muscle relaxation or guided imagery, can also be helpful in reducing stress and fostering mental clarity.

Mindful compassion:

Extend compassion and kindness to yourself and others. Practice self-compassion by treating yourself with understanding and acceptance, especially during times of self-doubt or struggle. Cultivate compassion for others by listening empathetically, offering support, and practicing forgiveness. By embodying a mindful attitude of compassion, you create an environment of positivity, understanding, and mental clarity.

Regular retreats or mindful retreat days:

Consider scheduling regular retreats or dedicated mindful retreat days in your calendar. These retreats can be a time for deep introspection, rejuvenation, and reconnecting with your inner self. Whether it's a weekend getaway to a peaceful location or a day spent in solitude at home, retreats provide an opportunity to disconnect from the noise of everyday life and immerse yourself in mindful practices such as meditation, reflection, and self-care. These retreats serve as a reset button, allowing you to recharge your mental clarity and gain fresh perspectives on life.

Mindful nature connection:

Spending time in nature is a powerful way to cultivate mental clarity. Take regular walks in natural settings, immerse yourself in the beauty of the outdoors, and engage your senses fully. Observe the sights, sounds, and textures of nature, and let yourself be present in the moment. Connecting with nature can bring a sense of peace, awe, and perspective, allowing your mind to quiet and your clarity to deepen.

Mindful visualization:

Practice mindful visualization techniques to enhance mental clarity. Close your eyes and imagine yourself in a calm and serene setting, such as a beach or a peaceful garden. Engage all your senses in this visualization, imagining the sights, sounds, smells, and even the sensations on your skin. Visualization can help quiet the mind, reduce overthinking, and promote a state of clarity and focus.

Mindful reflection:

At the end of each day, take a few moments to reflect on your experiences and emotions. Journal about the highlights and challenges of the day, allowing yourself to process and release any lingering thoughts or worries. This reflective practice promotes self-awareness and mental clarity, enabling you to gain insights and learn from your daily experiences.

Mindful reading:

Engage in mindful reading practices by selecting books that inspire and nourish your mind. Slow down your reading pace, savoring each word and sentence. Pause to reflect on the ideas presented and how they resonate with your own experiences. Mindful reading allows you to fully immerse yourself in the wisdom and knowledge shared in the pages, promoting mental clarity and expanding your perspective.

Mindful boundary setting:

Establish clear boundaries in your personal and professional life to protect your mental clarity. Learn to say no to activities or commitments that don't align with your values or priorities. Prioritize self-care and allocate time for rest, relaxation, and activities that bring you joy. By setting boundaries, you create space for mental clarity to thrive and prevent overwhelm and overthinking.

Mindful silence:

Embrace moments of silence throughout your day. Whether it's a few minutes of sitting quietly or practicing a silent walk, allow yourself to experience the power of silence. In the absence of external noise and distractions, you can tune in to your inner thoughts, emotions, and intuition. This practice cultivates mental clarity and helps you tap into your inner wisdom.

Mindful reflection questions:

Ask yourself reflective questions to deepen your self-awareness and promote mental clarity. Examples of mindful reflection questions include:

- What am I grateful for at this moment?

- How can I approach this situation with more mindfulness?

- What are my core values, and am I aligning my actions with them?

- What can I let go of to create more mental space and clarity?

- How can I bring more kindness and compassion into my interactions?

By regularly engaging in mindful reflection, you can gain valuable insights, clarify your priorities, and cultivate a clear and focused mind.

Conclusion:

Cultivating mindful habits is a transformative journey that can lead to sustained mental clarity, inner peace, and overall well-being. By incorporating these practices into your daily life, you can navigate the challenges of overthinking and nurture a mind that is present, focused, and calm. Remember, it's not about perfection.

Chapter 32: Strategies for overcoming overthinking in relationships.

―――

Introduction:

Relationships play a crucial role in our lives, but they can also become a breeding ground for overthinking and anxiety. Whether it's a romantic partnership, a friendship, or a family relationship, overthinking can create unnecessary stress and strain on our connections. In this chapter, we will explore strategies for overcoming overthinking in relationships and fostering healthier, more fulfilling connections.

Open communication:

One of the most effective strategies for overcoming overthinking in relationships is open and honest communication. Instead of making assumptions or jumping to conclusions, express your thoughts, concerns, and feelings directly to the other person. Clear and open communication helps to dispel misunderstandings, build trust, and promote a deeper understanding of each other's perspectives.

Practice mindful listening:

When engaging in conversations with your loved ones, practice mindful listening. Be fully present, giving your undivided attention to the speaker. Avoid interrupting or formulating responses in your mind while the other person is speaking. Instead, focus on truly understanding their words, emotions, and intentions. Mindful listening enhances connection and reduces overthinking by allowing for clearer and more authentic communication.

Challenge assumptions:

Overthinking often arises from making assumptions about others' thoughts, intentions, or behaviors. Challenge these assumptions by seeking clarification.

Instead of dwelling on your own interpretations, ask questions and engage in open dialogue to gain a better understanding of the other person's perspective. By challenging assumptions, you can prevent overthinking from hijacking your relationships.

Practice empathy:

Empathy is a powerful tool for overcoming overthinking in relationships. Put yourself in the other person's shoes and try to understand their emotions, experiences, and motivations. Cultivate empathy by actively listening, acknowledging their feelings, and validating their experiences. Empathy fosters compassion and connection, reducing overthinking and promoting healthier interactions.

Set boundaries:

Establishing clear boundaries is crucial for maintaining healthy relationships and preventing overthinking. Communicate your needs and expectations to the other person, and respectfully ask for what you require in terms of personal space, time, or emotional support. Setting boundaries creates a sense of safety and clarity, reducing overthinking and promoting a healthier dynamic.

Practice self-reflection:

Engage in self-reflection to gain insight into your own patterns of overthinking in relationships. Ask yourself why certain situations trigger overthinking and examine any underlying fears or insecurities. By understanding yourself better, you can address the root causes of overthinking and develop strategies to overcome it. Self-reflection also helps you take responsibility for your own thoughts and reactions, fostering healthier communication and connection.

Focus on the present moment:

Overthinking often stems from dwelling on the past or worrying about the future. Practice mindfulness to anchor yourself in the present moment. When spending time with your loved ones, be fully present and attentive, letting go of distractions and preoccupations. By focusing on the here and now, you can reduce overthinking and cultivate a deeper sense of connection and enjoyment in your relationships.

Cultivate trust:

Trust is the foundation of healthy relationships. If overthinking is driven by a lack of trust, consciously work on building and strengthening trust with your loved ones. Keep your commitments, be reliable, and demonstrate consistency in your words and actions. Cultivate trust by being honest, transparent, and accountable. Trust allows for a more secure and harmonious relationship, minimizing overthinking and promoting emotional well-being.

Practice self-care:

Taking care of yourself is essential for maintaining healthy relationships and reducing overthinking. Prioritize self-care activities that nurture your mental, emotional, and physical well-being. Engage in activities that bring you joy, practice stress management techniques, and ensure you have adequate time for rest and relaxation. When you prioritize self-care, you are better equipped to approach your relationships with a clear and balanced mindset, reducing the tendency to overthink.

Let go of control:

Overthinking in relationships can often stem from a desire to control outcomes or the behavior of others. Recognize that you cannot control everything or everyone in your relationships. Instead, focus on what you can control—your own thoughts, actions, and responses. Practice acceptance and surrender to the natural flow of relationships, allowing space for growth and mutual understanding.

Seek support:

If overthinking in relationships becomes overwhelming, don't hesitate to seek support from trusted friends, family, or even a therapist. Sharing your concerns and thoughts with others can provide valuable insights and perspectives. A supportive network can offer guidance, reassurance, and help you navigate through challenging relationship dynamics.

Letting go of past hurts:

Past hurts or unresolved conflicts can fuel overthinking in relationships. Practice forgiveness and letting go of grudges to free yourself from the weight of the past. It's important to acknowledge the pain but also make a conscious choice to release it and move forward. This allows space for healing, growth, and the development of healthier relationship patterns.

Focus on collaboration:

Instead of viewing relationships as a battleground or a series of power struggles, shift your mindset towards collaboration and teamwork. Recognize that you and your loved ones are on the same side, working together to foster connection and understanding. Embrace a cooperative approach that values compromise, empathy, and mutual growth.

Practice gratitude:

Gratitude is a powerful antidote to overthinking and negativity in relationships. Take time each day to reflect on the things you appreciate about your loved ones. Express gratitude for their presence, support, and positive qualities. This practice shifts your focus from overthinking to acknowledging the positive aspects of your relationships, fostering a healthier and more optimistic mindset.

Accept imperfections:

No relationship is perfect, and accepting this reality can alleviate overthinking. Understand that both you and your loved ones are human, with flaws and imperfections. Embrace the imperfections as part of the journey and focus on nurturing the strengths and connection within the relationship. Cultivating acceptance allows for a more compassionate and balanced perspective, reducing overthinking.

Engage in shared activities:

Participating in shared activities and experiences can strengthen bonds and reduce overthinking in relationships. Find common interests or hobbies that you can enjoy together. Engaging in these activities creates opportunities for positive interactions, laughter, and shared memories, fostering a deeper sense of connection and reducing overthinking.

Practice self-validation:

Overthinking often arises from seeking validation from others. Learn to validate yourself and trust your own instincts and feelings. Recognize your own worth and value, independent of external validation. When you cultivate self-validation, you rely less on the opinions and actions of others, reducing overthinking and promoting healthier relationships.

Celebrate individuality:

In relationships, it's important to honor and celebrate each other's individuality. Avoid comparing yourself or your loved ones to others, as it can fuel overthinking and create unnecessary pressure. Embrace and appreciate the unique qualities, strengths, and perspectives that each person brings to the relationship. Celebrating individuality fosters acceptance, understanding, and a deeper connection.

Practice patience:

Overthinking can lead to impatience and a constant need for reassurance or immediate resolutions. Practice patience in your relationships, understanding that growth, understanding, and resolution take time. Trust in the process and allow space for open communication, reflection, and growth. Patience promotes a calmer and more balanced approach to relationships, reducing overthinking.

Prioritize emotional well-being:

Above all, prioritize your emotional well-being in relationships. By prioritizing your emotional well-being in relationships, you create a foundation of self-care and self-awareness that helps to combat overthinking. Take time for self-reflection, journaling, or engaging in activities that promote emotional balance and inner peace. By nurturing your own emotional well-being, you are better equipped to engage in healthy and fulfilling relationships.

Conclusion:

Overthinking in relationships can create unnecessary stress, strain, and misunderstandings. However, by implementing these strategies, you can overcome overthinking and foster healthier connections with your loved ones. Remember to prioritize open communication, empathy, self-reflection, and self-care. Embrace the present moment, let go of control, and practice gratitude and acceptance. With these strategies, you can cultivate a mindset that is focused, compassionate, and free from the burdens of overthinking, allowing your relationships to thrive and flourish.

Chapter 33: Letting go of control and embracing acceptance.

———

Introduction:

In our quest for certainty and security, we often find ourselves trying to control every aspect of our lives. This need for control can manifest in various areas, including relationships, career, and personal goals. However, excessive control can lead to stress, anxiety, and even strained relationships. In this chapter, we will explore the importance of letting go of control and embracing acceptance as a pathway to inner peace and fulfillment.

Understanding the illusion of control:

The desire for control stems from a fundamental need for security and predictability. However, it is important to recognize that control is often an illusion. Life is inherently unpredictable, and there are many factors beyond our control. Trying to control every outcome can lead to frustration and disappointment. Embracing the idea that some things are beyond our control allows us to focus on what we can influence and accept the rest.

Surrendering to the present moment:

One of the keys to letting go of control is learning to surrender to the present moment. Often, we get caught up in ruminating about the past or worrying about the future. By bringing our awareness to the present moment, we can cultivate a sense of acceptance and peace. Practice mindfulness and meditation to develop the skill of being fully present and letting go of the need to control every aspect of your life.

Embracing uncertainty:

Uncertainty is a natural part of life. Rather than resisting it, learn to embrace it. Recognize that uncertainty can bring opportunities for growth, learning, and new experiences. By accepting uncertainty, you open yourself up to new possibilities and reduce the need for excessive control. Embrace the adventure of life and see uncertainty as a chance to step out of your comfort zone and explore new horizons.

Trusting the process:

Letting go of control requires trust—trust in yourself, trust in others, and trust in the unfolding of life. Trust that things will work out as they are meant to, even if they don't align with your initial plans or expectations. Trust that you have the inner resources to navigate challenges and make the best choices in each moment. Cultivate a sense of faith and trust in the process of life, and you will find greater peace and acceptance.

Practicing non-attachment:

Attachment to specific outcomes or expectations can create a sense of rigidity and control. Practice non-attachment by letting go of fixed expectations and being open to various possibilities. This doesn't mean giving up on your goals or dreams but rather detaching from the specific way they manifest. By embracing non-attachment, you can adapt to changing circumstances and find joy in the journey rather than fixating on a predetermined destination.

Developing flexibility:

Letting go of control involves developing flexibility in your thinking and actions. Be open to alternative perspectives, ideas, and approaches. Flexibility allows you to adapt to changing situations and find creative solutions. Cultivate a mindset that embraces change and sees it as an opportunity for growth and self-discovery. The more flexible you become, the less you feel the need to control every aspect of your life.

Cultivating self-trust:

Letting go of control requires developing a strong sense of self-trust. Trust in your own abilities, intuition, and decision-making process. Recognize that you are capable of handling whatever challenges come your way. Building self-trust allows you to release the need for external validation and rely on your own judgment and inner wisdom.

Embracing acceptance:

Acceptance is a powerful tool for letting go of control. Acceptance does not mean passivity or resignation but rather acknowledging and embracing reality as it is. Acceptance allows you to let go of resistance and surrender to the flow of life. It means accepting both the positive and negative aspects of life without judgment or attachment. When you embrace acceptance, you free yourself from the burden of trying to control every outcome and instead learn to navigate life with grace and equanimity.

Practicing mindful detachment:

Mindful detachment is about observing your thoughts, emotions, and circumstances without getting entangled in them. It involves cultivating a sense of spaciousness and perspective, allowing you to detach from the need to control every situation. By practicing mindful detachment, you can maintain a sense of inner calm and clarity even in the face of uncertainty.

Letting go of perfectionism:

Perfectionism is often driven by a need for control. By letting go of perfectionism and embracing imperfections, you open yourself up to greater self-acceptance and self-compassion. Recognize that perfection is an unattainable goal and that mistakes and failures are valuable opportunities for growth and learning. Embrace the beauty of imperfection and allow yourself to be human.

Cultivating gratitude:

Gratitude is a powerful practice that helps shift our focus from what we lack to what we have. By cultivating gratitude, you develop a sense of contentment and appreciation for the present moment. It allows you to let go of the need to control and instead embrace the abundance and blessings in your life. Practice gratitude daily by reflecting on the things you are grateful for, no matter how small.

Seeking support:

Letting go of control can be challenging, especially if you have developed a pattern of overthinking and excessive control. Seek support from trusted friends, family members, or even a therapist or coach who can provide guidance and help you navigate this process. Surround yourself with a supportive network of people who understand and respect your journey toward letting go of control.

Conclusion:

Letting go of control and embracing acceptance is a transformative process that requires self-awareness, mindfulness, and practice. It is about releasing the grip on outcomes, surrendering to the present moment, and trusting in the inherent wisdom of life. By letting go of control, you create space for peace, joy, and fulfillment. Embrace the beauty of uncertainty, cultivate flexibility, and nourish a sense of gratitude and acceptance. As you embark on this journey, remember that it is a continuous practice, and each step forward brings you closer to living a life of freedom, authenticity, and inner harmony.

Chapter 34: Mindful technology use for improved mental clarity.

———

I ntroduction:

In today's digital age, technology has become an integral part of our lives. We rely on smartphones, tablets, computers, and other devices for communication, information, and entertainment. While technology offers many benefits, it can also contribute to overstimulation, distraction, and a constant influx of information that can overwhelm our minds. In this chapter, we will explore the concept of mindful technology use and how it can help improve mental clarity.

Understanding the impact of technology on mental clarity:

Technology has the power to both enhance and hinder our mental clarity. On one hand, it provides access to a wealth of knowledge, tools for productivity, and platforms for connection. On the other hand, excessive use of technology can lead to information overload, decreased focus, and a constant need for external stimulation. It is crucial to recognize and understand the impact technology has on our mental well-being.

Practicing digital mindfulness:

Digital mindfulness involves being intentional and aware of how we engage with technology. It means using technology with purpose and consciously choosing when and how to engage with digital devices. Practicing digital mindfulness helps us create boundaries, reduce distractions, and maintain mental clarity amidst the constant stream of information.

Setting technology boundaries:

Setting boundaries around technology use is essential for maintaining mental clarity. This includes establishing designated technology-free zones or times, such as during meals or before bedtime. Setting limits on social media usage, notifications, and screen time can help prevent overwhelm and allow for more focused and intentional technology use.

Cultivating a digital detox:

Periodically disconnecting from technology through a digital detox can be highly beneficial for mental clarity. A digital detox involves taking a break from all digital devices and platforms for a designated period, allowing the mind to recharge, reset, and regain focus. It provides an opportunity to reconnect with oneself, nature, and the present moment.

Mindful consumption of digital content:

Being mindful of the digital content we consume is crucial for mental clarity. It involves consciously choosing high-quality, informative, and uplifting content while limiting exposure to negativity, sensationalism, and excessive consumption. Selecting content that aligns with our values and interests can enhance mental well-being and prevent information overload.

Utilizing technology for mindfulness practices:

While technology can sometimes be a source of distraction, it can also be a tool for mindfulness practices. Various smartphone apps, websites, and wearable devices offer guided meditations, breathing exercises, and relaxation techniques that can support mental clarity. Embracing technology mindfully in this way allows us to harness its potential for well-being.

Creating digital organization systems:

Digital clutter can contribute to mental clutter and overwhelm. Creating digital organization systems, such as decluttering files and emails, organizing apps and bookmarks, and utilizing productivity tools, can help streamline our digital environment. A clean and organized digital space promotes mental clarity and reduces the cognitive load associated with digital disarray.

Practicing digital mindfulness in relationships:

Technology has also changed the way we communicate and connect with others. It is important to practice digital mindfulness in our relationships by being fully present and attentive when engaging in digital conversations. Setting boundaries around technology use during face-to-face interactions and prioritizing real-time connections fosters deeper connections and enhances mental clarity.

Engaging in offline activities:

To balance the time spent with technology, it is important to engage in offline activities that promote mental clarity. This includes pursuing hobbies, spending time in nature, practicing mindfulness meditation, engaging in physical exercise, and connecting with loved ones without the interference of digital devices. These activities provide opportunities for rejuvenation, self-reflection, and deepening of personal connections.

Reflecting on the impact of technology:

Regularly reflecting on the impact of technology on our mental clarity is essential. This reflection allows us to assess how technology use aligns with our values, goals, and overall well-being. It also helps us identify any unhealthy patterns or dependencies on technology that may be negatively affecting our mental clarity.

Developing healthy technology habits:

Building healthy technology habits is crucial for maintaining mental clarity. This involves being mindful of our digital behaviors and consciously choosing habits that support our well-being. For example, we can establish a regular technology-free time in our daily routine, practice digital mindfulness before engaging with technology, and prioritize offline activities that nourish our mind and body.

Practicing digital sabbaticals:

In addition to periodic digital detoxes, taking longer breaks from technology through digital sabbaticals can be highly beneficial. This involves intentionally disconnecting from technology for an extended period, such as a weekend or a vacation. During this time, we can engage in activities that promote relaxation, reflection, and deep connection with ourselves and others.

Embracing slow technology movement:

The slow technology movement emphasizes the importance of slowing down and being intentional in our use of technology. It encourages us to question the constant need for speed, instant gratification, and constant connectivity. By embracing the principles of the slow technology movement, we can cultivate a more mindful and intentional relationship with technology, allowing for increased mental clarity.

Seeking support and accountability:

Changing our technology habits and striving for mindful technology use can be challenging. Seeking support from others who share similar goals or joining online communities focused on digital well-being can provide valuable guidance and accountability. Connecting with like-minded individuals can inspire us to stay committed to our intentions and share experiences and strategies for maintaining mental clarity.

Modeling mindful technology use:

If we want to encourage mindful technology use in our families, workplaces, and communities, it is important to lead by example. Modeling healthy technology habits, setting boundaries, and prioritizing offline connections can inspire others to reflect on their own technology use and strive for greater mental clarity. By being mindful of our own technology behaviors, we can create a positive ripple effect in our surroundings.

Conclusion:

Mindful technology use is a powerful tool for improving mental clarity in the digital age. By understanding the impact of technology, setting boundaries, practicing digital mindfulness, and engaging in offline activities, we can harness the benefits of technology while maintaining a clear and focused mind. It is essential to cultivate a healthy relationship with technology, where we are in control of its influence on our mental well-being. Through conscious choices and intentional habits, we can navigate the digital landscape with clarity, balance, and mindfulness.

Chapter 35: Strategies for overcoming overthinking at work.

———

I ntroduction:

Work can often be a breeding ground for overthinking. The pressures, deadlines, and constant flow of information can overwhelm our minds, leading to stress, anxiety, and decreased productivity. In this chapter, we will explore effective strategies for overcoming overthinking at work, enabling us to find clarity, focus, and peace of mind in our professional lives.

Recognizing overthinking patterns:

The first step in overcoming overthinking at work is to recognize the patterns and triggers that lead to excessive rumination. Pay attention to the situations, tasks, or interactions that tend to trigger overthinking. By becoming aware of these patterns, you can take proactive measures to address them.

Setting clear goals and priorities:

Having clear goals and priorities is crucial for managing overthinking at work. Define your objectives and break them down into manageable tasks. This will help you stay focused and prevent your mind from wandering into unproductive thoughts. Regularly review and adjust your goals to ensure they align with your long-term vision.

Practicing time management:

Effective time management is a key strategy for overcoming overthinking at work. Create a schedule or to-do list that outlines your tasks and deadlines. Prioritize your work based on importance and urgency. By allocating specific time slots for different activities, you can maintain focus and avoid the tendency to overthink.

Embracing mindful work practices:

Incorporating mindfulness into your work routine can significantly reduce overthinking. Take short breaks throughout the day to engage in mindful practices such as deep breathing, meditation, or stretching. These practices help calm the mind, increase self-awareness, and improve concentration.

Adopting a growth mindset:

A growth mindset is essential for overcoming overthinking at work. Embrace challenges as opportunities for growth and learning. Instead of fearing failure or obsessing over perfection, view setbacks as stepping stones to success. Cultivate a positive mindset that values progress and resilience.

Seeking support and collaboration:

Don't hesitate to seek support and collaborate with colleagues. Discussing challenges, brainstorming ideas, and sharing perspectives can provide valuable insights and help break free from overthinking. Build a supportive network within your workplace that encourages open communication and problem-solving.

Establishing boundaries:

Setting boundaries is crucial for maintaining a healthy work-life balance and preventing overthinking. Clearly define your working hours and create a separation between work and personal life. Avoid checking work emails or engaging in work-related tasks during your leisure time. This allows you to recharge and disconnect from work-related thoughts.

Practicing self-care:

Self-care plays a vital role in overcoming overthinking at work. Prioritize activities that promote physical and mental well-being, such as exercise, proper nutrition, and sufficient sleep. Engage in hobbies, spend time with loved ones, and take regular breaks to rejuvenate your mind and prevent burnout.

Challenging negative thoughts:

Overthinking often involves negative thoughts and self-doubt. Challenge these thoughts by examining the evidence and considering alternative perspectives. Replace negative self-talk with positive affirmations and focus on your strengths and accomplishments. Practice self-compassion and remind yourself that mistakes and setbacks are a natural part of the learning process.

Cultivating a positive work environment:

Creating a positive work environment is instrumental in overcoming overthinking. Foster a culture of open communication, respect, and support within your team. Encourage collaboration and celebrate achievements. By cultivating a positive work atmosphere, you can reduce stress and promote a more productive and enjoyable work experience.

Conclusion:

Overcoming overthinking at work requires a combination of self-awareness, proactive strategies, and a supportive work environment. By recognizing overthinking patterns, setting clear goals, practicing mindfulness, seeking support, and practicing self-care, you can effectively manage overthinking and improve your overall well-being and productivity at work. Remember that it takes time and practice to break free from overthinking habits, so be patient and kind to yourself throughout the process.

In addition to the strategies mentioned above, there are a few more techniques you can employ to overcome overthinking at work:

Implementing a daily reflection practice: Take a few minutes at the end of each workday to reflect on your accomplishments and identify areas for improvement. This practice allows you to acknowledge your achievements and gain perspective on your progress, reducing the tendency to dwell on negative thoughts or excessive analysis.

Embracing positive visualization: Visualize successful outcomes and positive experiences related to your work. Imagine yourself completing tasks with ease, receiving positive feedback, and achieving your goals. Positive visualization can help shift your mindset from overthinking to a more optimistic and solution-oriented perspective.

Practicing active listening: Effective communication is essential in the workplace. Practice active listening by fully engaging in conversations and focusing on the speaker's words and non-verbal cues. This not only enhances your understanding but also prevents overthinking about potential misinterpretations or conflicts.

Taking regular breaks: Give yourself permission to take regular breaks throughout the workday. Stepping away from your desk, going for a walk, or engaging in a brief relaxation exercise can help clear your mind and reduce mental fatigue. These breaks provide valuable opportunities to reset and recharge, enhancing your ability to approach tasks with clarity and focus.

Implementing a digital detox: In today's digital age, it's easy to become overwhelmed by constant notifications, emails, and information overload. Consider implementing a digital detox by setting specific time periods where you disconnect from technology. This break from digital distractions allows you to regain mental clarity and reduce the urge to constantly check for updates or respond to messages.

Seeking feedback and learning opportunities: View feedback as an opportunity for growth rather than criticism. Seek constructive feedback from colleagues or supervisors to gain different perspectives and improve your performance. Actively pursue learning opportunities, such as attending workshops or conferences, to enhance your skills and knowledge. By focusing on growth and development, you can redirect your energy away from overthinking.

Practicing gratitude: Cultivate a sense of gratitude for the work you have and the opportunities it provides. Take a moment each day to reflect on the aspects of your job that you appreciate, such as supportive colleagues, interesting projects, or personal growth. Gratitude helps shift your focus from overthinking and negativity to a more positive mindset.

Engaging in physical activity: Regular physical activity has numerous benefits for mental clarity and overall well-being. Find ways to incorporate exercise into your work routine, such as taking walking meetings or utilizing your lunch break for a quick workout. Physical activity releases endorphins, reduces stress, and boosts cognitive function, helping to combat overthinking.

Remember, overcoming overthinking at work is a gradual process that requires consistency and self-awareness. Experiment with different strategies and techniques to find what works best for you. Be patient and compassionate with yourself as you navigate through the challenges, and celebrate your progress along the way.

By implementing these strategies, you can cultivate a healthier mindset, improve your work performance, and find greater satisfaction in your professional life. Break free from the grips of overthinking and enjoy a more balanced and fulfilling work experience.

Chapter 36: Exploring the benefits of meditation for mental clarity.

Introduction:

In today's fast-paced world, finding moments of calm and mental clarity can be challenging. Our minds are often filled with thoughts, worries, and distractions, leading to increased stress and overthinking. However, one powerful practice that can help calm the mind and enhance mental clarity is meditation. In this chapter, we will explore the benefits of meditation and how it can contribute to overcoming overthinking and achieving a state of mental clarity.

Understanding meditation:

Meditation is a practice that involves focusing the mind and achieving a state of deep relaxation and heightened awareness. It has been practiced for thousands of years and is rooted in various traditions, including Buddhism, Hinduism, and Taoism. Meditation techniques can vary, but they typically involve directing attention to a specific object, such as the breath, a mantra, or a visualization, while observing thoughts and emotions without judgment.

Calming the mind and reducing overthinking:

One of the primary benefits of meditation is its ability to calm the mind and reduce overthinking. By consciously directing your attention to the present moment, you can interrupt the cycle of repetitive thoughts and worries. Through regular meditation practice, you develop the skill of observing thoughts without getting caught up in them, allowing you to gain mental clarity and a greater sense of peace.

Enhancing emotional well-being:

Meditation can also have a profound impact on emotional well-being. By cultivating mindfulness and self-awareness through meditation, you become more attuned to your emotions and can respond to them in a more balanced way. This can help you break free from negative thought patterns and reduce the emotional reactivity that often accompanies overthinking.

Improving concentration and focus:

Overthinking can scatter our attention and make it challenging to concentrate on tasks at hand. Meditation can enhance concentration and focus by training the mind to stay present and resist distractions. With regular practice, you develop the ability to sustain attention for longer periods, leading to improved productivity and efficiency in both personal and professional endeavors.

Reducing stress and enhancing resilience:

Stress is a common trigger for overthinking, and it can take a toll on both mental and physical well-being. Meditation has been shown to reduce stress levels by activating the body's relaxation response and lowering the production of stress hormones. By incorporating meditation into your routine, you can build resilience and better cope with the challenges and uncertainties of life.

Cultivating self-compassion:

Overthinking often involves self-criticism and judgment. Meditation provides an opportunity to cultivate self-compassion and self-acceptance. As you practice observing your thoughts without judgment, you develop a kind and non-reactive attitude towards yourself. This self-compassion can help break the cycle of overthinking and foster a more positive and nurturing inner dialogue.

Enhancing cognitive function:

Research has shown that meditation can have positive effects on cognitive function, including memory, attention, and problem-solving skills. By training the mind to focus and stay present, meditation enhances cognitive abilities and supports mental clarity. This can have a direct impact on productivity and decision-making in various aspects of life.

Promoting physical well-being:

The benefits of meditation extend beyond mental and emotional well-being. Regular meditation practice has been associated with numerous physical health benefits, such as reduced blood pressure, improved immune function, and better sleep. When your body is in a state of balance and vitality, it positively influences your mental clarity and ability to manage overthinking.

Conclusion:

Meditation is a powerful tool for cultivating mental clarity and overcoming overthinking. By incorporating regular meditation practice into your life, you can experience the numerous benefits it offers, including a calm mind, enhanced emotional well-being, improved concentration, and greater resilience. The practice of meditation allows you to step back from the constant stream of thoughts and enter a state of deep relaxation and inner stillness. Through mindfulness and self-awareness, you develop the capacity to observe your thoughts without attachment or judgment.

As you continue to deepen your meditation practice, you may notice that the overthinking patterns that once consumed your mind start to lose their grip. The incessant mental chatter begins to quiet down, and you gain a newfound clarity and peace within.

To make the most of your meditation practice, here are some tips to consider:

Consistency: Aim for regularity in your practice. Set aside a specific time each day to meditate, even if it's just a few minutes. Consistency is key to experiencing the long-term benefits of meditation.

Start small: If you're new to meditation, begin with shorter sessions and gradually increase the duration as you become more comfortable. It's better to start with a few minutes of focused meditation than to force yourself into longer sessions that feel overwhelming.

Find a comfortable position: Whether you choose to sit cross-legged on a cushion, in a chair with your feet planted firmly on the ground, or even lie down, find a position that allows you to be relaxed and alert. The goal is to be comfortable while maintaining a posture that supports wakefulness.

Focus on the breath: The breath is a common object of meditation because it is always present and easily accessible. Direct your attention to the sensation of the breath entering and leaving your body. When your mind wanders, gently bring it back to the breath without judgment.

Explore guided meditations: If you find it challenging to meditate on your own, consider using guided meditations. There are numerous apps, websites, and resources available that provide guided audio recordings to support your practice.

Be patient and gentle with yourself: Meditation is a practice, and like any skill, it takes time and patience to develop. Be kind to yourself as you navigate through moments of distraction or restlessness. Treat yourself with compassion and know that each moment of meditation is an opportunity to learn and grow.

Remember, the goal of meditation is not to stop your thoughts entirely but rather to create a sense of spaciousness and clarity in your mind. Over time, as you cultivate a regular meditation practice, you will notice the benefits expanding into various aspects of your life.

In conclusion, meditation is a powerful tool for breaking free from overthinking and cultivating mental clarity. By incorporating the practice into your daily routine, you can experience a greater sense of calm, focus, and resilience. Embrace the journey of meditation, and allow yourself to discover the transformative effects it can have on your mind, body, and overall well-being.

Chapter 37: Strengthening emotional intelligence to combat overthinking.

Introduction:

Emotional intelligence plays a crucial role in our ability to navigate and manage our emotions effectively. It encompasses the awareness, understanding, and regulation of our own emotions, as well as the ability to empathize with and relate to the emotions of others. When it comes to combating overthinking, developing and strengthening emotional intelligence can be a powerful tool. In this chapter, we will explore various strategies and techniques to enhance emotional intelligence, enabling you to break free from overthinking patterns and cultivate mental clarity.

Self-awareness:

Self-awareness is the foundation of emotional intelligence. It involves recognizing and understanding your own emotions, thoughts, and behaviors. By developing a keen sense of self-awareness, you can become more attuned to the triggers and patterns that contribute to overthinking. Take time to reflect on your emotions and thoughts without judgment, and pay attention to how they influence your decision-making and overall well-being.

Emotional regulation:

Emotional regulation refers to the ability to manage and regulate your emotions in a healthy and constructive manner. It involves recognizing and acknowledging your emotions without being overwhelmed by them. Practice techniques such as deep breathing, mindfulness, and grounding exercises to help you stay centered and calm in the face of challenging emotions. By regulating your emotions effectively, you can prevent them from spiraling into overthinking.

Empathy:

Empathy is the ability to understand and share the feelings of others. By developing empathy, you can enhance your interpersonal relationships and improve your communication skills. Engage in active listening and strive to understand the perspectives and emotions of those around you. This will not only foster deeper connections but also help you gain valuable insights into different viewpoints, reducing the need for overthinking and promoting clarity.

Emotional awareness in others:

In addition to understanding your own emotions, it's important to be attuned to the emotions of others. Pay attention to non-verbal cues, such as facial expressions and body language, to better understand how others are feeling. This heightened emotional awareness can prevent misunderstandings, build stronger relationships, and reduce the need to overthink social interactions.

Practicing empathetic communication:

Effective communication is essential for managing relationships and reducing overthinking. Practice empathetic communication by actively listening, validating others' emotions, and expressing your own thoughts and feelings in a clear and respectful manner. Cultivating empathetic communication skills can help create an open and supportive environment, reducing the need for overthinking and promoting healthy dialogue.

Developing emotional resilience:

Emotional resilience refers to the ability to bounce back from adversity and cope with challenges. It involves maintaining a positive outlook, managing stress effectively, and adapting to change. Building emotional resilience can help you navigate difficult situations without getting stuck in overthinking. Practice self-care, seek support when needed, and cultivate a growth mindset to develop emotional resilience.

Cultivating positive relationships:

Healthy and supportive relationships contribute to emotional well-being and can help reduce overthinking. Surround yourself with people who uplift and encourage you. Foster relationships built on trust, respect, and open communication. By nurturing positive relationships, you create a support system that can provide valuable perspective and help you gain clarity in times of uncertainty.

Practicing mindful decision-making:

Mindful decision-making involves making choices based on self-awareness, emotional intelligence, and a clear understanding of your values and goals. Instead of getting caught up in overthinking every decision, practice mindfulness by focusing on the present moment, considering all relevant information, and trusting your intuition. Mindful decision-making can help you make choices that align with your authentic self and reduce the need for excessive analysis.

Conclusion:

Strengthening emotional intelligence is a powerful approach to combating overthinking and cultivating mental clarity. By developing self-awareness, emotional regulation, empathy, and emotional resilience, you can gain control over your thoughts and emotions, reducing the tendency to overthink. Additionally, practicing empathetic communication and cultivating positive relationships can create an environment that supports open dialogue and understanding, minimizing the need for excessive rumination.

Mindful decision-making is another important aspect of emotional intelligence. By staying present, considering your values and goals, and trusting your intuition, you can make decisions with greater confidence and clarity. This approach allows you to let go of the need for perfection and embrace the idea that there is no one "right" answer. Instead, you focus on making choices that align with your authentic self and move you forward.

In addition to these strategies, incorporating mindfulness practices such as meditation into your daily routine can further enhance your emotional intelligence and reduce overthinking. Mindfulness helps you stay grounded in the present moment, observe your thoughts without judgment, and cultivate a sense of calm and clarity.

It's important to note that developing emotional intelligence is a lifelong journey. It requires consistent practice, self-reflection, and a willingness to learn and grow. Be patient with yourself and celebrate small victories along the way. Each step you take towards strengthening your emotional intelligence brings you closer to breaking free from the trap of overthinking.

Remember, overcoming overthinking is not about eliminating thoughts altogether, but rather developing a healthier relationship with them. With emotional intelligence as your guide, you can navigate the challenges of overthinking with greater ease, leading to a more peaceful and clear state of mind.

In conclusion, Chapter 37 emphasizes the significance of strengthening emotional intelligence to combat overthinking. By cultivating self-awareness, empathy, emotional regulation, and resilience, and practicing mindful decision-making and communication, you can break free from the cycle of overthinking. The journey towards enhanced emotional intelligence requires dedication and self-reflection, but the rewards are well worth it—a greater sense of clarity, improved relationships, and a more balanced and fulfilling life. Embrace the strategies outlined in this chapter, and let them empower you to navigate the complexities of your thoughts and emotions with wisdom and grace.

Chapter 38: Strategies for setting boundaries with overthinking triggers.

———

In our modern world filled with constant stimulation and information overload, it's crucial to set boundaries with the triggers that lead to overthinking. These triggers can be external factors such as social media, news, or demanding work environments, as well as internal factors like self-criticism and perfectionism. By establishing clear boundaries, you can regain control over your thoughts and prevent them from spiraling into excessive rumination.

One effective strategy for setting boundaries is to identify your personal overthinking triggers. Reflect on the situations, people, or activities that tend to ignite your overthinking tendencies. Is it certain conversations with specific individuals? Is it scrolling through social media for too long? Is it taking on too many responsibilities at once? Understanding your triggers is the first step towards setting boundaries.

Once you have identified your triggers, it's time to establish practical boundaries. Here are some strategies to consider:

Time limits: Set specific time limits for activities that tend to trigger overthinking. For example, allocate a certain amount of time each day for social media or news consumption and stick to it. This helps prevent mindless scrolling or getting caught up in negativity.

Prioritization: Learn to prioritize your tasks and responsibilities. Determine what truly needs your attention and energy, and be willing to say no to tasks or commitments that are not aligned with your goals or values. Setting clear boundaries around your time and energy helps prevent overwhelm and excessive rumination.

Communication: Communicate your boundaries to others. Let your friends, family, and colleagues know about your need for personal space and time to recharge. Clearly express your limits and expectations, and assertively communicate when something crosses those boundaries. Effective communication is essential for maintaining healthy relationships and reducing overthinking triggers.

Self-care rituals: Establish self-care practices that nurture your well-being and provide a mental and emotional break from overthinking. This could include activities such as meditation, exercise, journaling, spending time in nature, or engaging in creative pursuits. Carving out time for self-care allows you to recharge and create a buffer against overthinking triggers.

Setting work-life boundaries: In today's always-connected work culture, it's crucial to establish boundaries between work and personal life. Create designated work hours and honor your personal time. Avoid checking emails or engaging in work-related tasks during your off hours. Setting clear boundaries between work and personal life helps prevent burnout and allows for a healthier work-life balance.

Self-compassion: Practice self-compassion and self-acceptance when you find yourself slipping into overthinking patterns. Remember that it's natural to have thoughts and worries, but you have the power to choose how much attention and energy you give them. Treat yourself with kindness and understand that setting boundaries is a process that takes time and practice.

Create a supportive environment: Surround yourself with people who understand and respect your boundaries. Seek out individuals who encourage healthy thought patterns and support your journey in overcoming overthinking. Build a network of like-minded individuals who can provide guidance and accountability.

Remember, setting boundaries is not about being rigid or shutting yourself off from the world. It's about creating a healthy and balanced relationship with the triggers that contribute to overthinking. By establishing clear boundaries, you reclaim your power and create space for more intentional and mindful living.

In conclusion, Chapter 38 highlights the importance of setting boundaries with overthinking triggers. By identifying your triggers, prioritizing your time and energy, communicating your boundaries, practicing self-care, and cultivating self-compassion, you can effectively manage overthinking tendencies. Setting boundaries empowers you to take control of your thoughts and create a supportive environment that promotes mental clarity and well-being. Embrace these strategies and witness the transformative impact

Chapter 39: Cultivating gratitude in daily life for enhanced mental clarity.

In a world that often feels fast-paced and demanding, it's easy to get caught up in the whirlwind of daily challenges and overlook the blessings that surround us. However, cultivating gratitude can be a powerful practice for enhancing mental clarity and overall well-being. When we consciously focus on the things we are grateful for, we shift our perspective from scarcity to abundance, from negativity to positivity, and from overthinking to a state of calm and clarity.

Gratitude is the practice of acknowledging and appreciating the goodness in our lives, both big and small. It involves recognizing the positive aspects of our experiences, relationships, and surroundings, and expressing gratitude for them. By actively cultivating gratitude, we train our minds to become more attuned to the positive aspects of life, which can significantly impact our mental clarity and overall happiness.

Here are some strategies to help you cultivate gratitude in your daily life:

Gratitude journal: Set aside a few minutes each day to write down three things you are grateful for. They can be simple pleasures, moments of joy, acts of kindness, or anything else that brings a sense of gratitude. Writing them down helps solidify the experience and reinforces the positive emotions associated with gratitude.

Gratitude rituals: Incorporate gratitude into your daily rituals. For example, you can start your day by expressing gratitude for a good night's sleep, a warm cup of coffee, or the sunrise. You can also end your day by reflecting on the positive experiences or interactions you had throughout the day. Infusing gratitude into your rituals helps anchor the practice into your daily routine.

Mindful appreciation: Practice being present in the moment and notice the beauty and abundance around you. Whether it's the colors of nature, the laughter of loved ones, or the taste of a delicious meal, take a moment to fully appreciate and savor the experience. Mindful appreciation allows you to connect with the present moment and cultivate gratitude for the richness of life.

Gratitude letters: Take the time to write heartfelt letters expressing gratitude to the people who have positively impacted your life. It could be a family member, a friend, a mentor, or even a stranger who showed kindness. Expressing gratitude not only strengthens your relationships but also deepens your own sense of appreciation.

Acts of kindness: Engage in acts of kindness and service towards others. By extending kindness to others, we create a ripple effect of gratitude and positivity. Whether it's volunteering, helping a neighbor, or offering support to someone in need, these acts not only benefit others but also foster a sense of gratitude within ourselves.

Gratitude walks: Take a leisurely walk in nature and intentionally focus on the beauty and wonders around you. Notice the vibrant colors, the sounds of birds, the feel of the breeze on your skin. As you immerse yourself in the present moment and appreciate the natural world, you cultivate gratitude and mental clarity.

Gratitude reminders: Place visual reminders of gratitude in your living or working space. It could be a gratitude jar, where you write down and collect notes of things you're grateful for. Or you can create a gratitude board or collage with pictures or quotes that inspire feelings of gratitude. These reminders serve as prompts to shift your focus towards gratitude throughout the day.

Gratitude meditation: Incorporate gratitude into your meditation practice. During your meditation, reflect on the things you are grateful for and allow the feelings of gratitude to fill your heart and mind. This practice trains your brain to naturally lean towards gratitude and enhances your overall sense of well-being.

By consistently practicing gratitude, you can experience a multitude of benefits. Cultivating gratitude enhances your mental clarity by shifting your focus away from worries, regrets, and negative thoughts. Instead, it redirects your attention towards the positive aspects of life, creating a sense of appreciation and contentment. Here are some additional ways in which cultivating gratitude can enhance your mental clarity:

Stress reduction: Gratitude has been shown to reduce stress levels and promote relaxation. When you focus on the things you are grateful for, it shifts your perspective away from stressors and brings a sense of calm. This mental clarity allows you to approach challenges with a clearer and more focused mind.

Improved perspective: Gratitude helps you gain a broader perspective on life. It reminds you of the bigger picture and helps you recognize that setbacks and difficulties are often temporary. By focusing on what you are grateful for, you develop a more positive outlook, which can minimize the impact of overthinking and allow you to see opportunities and solutions more clearly.

Enhanced self-awareness: Cultivating gratitude requires you to pay attention to your thoughts, emotions, and experiences. This practice of self-reflection and self-awareness allows you to better understand yourself and your needs. By being aware of the things that bring you joy and gratitude, you can make choices and decisions that align with your values and bring you closer to mental clarity.

Increased resilience: Gratitude strengthens your resilience in the face of adversity. When you regularly acknowledge and appreciate the positive aspects of your life, it builds a reservoir of positive emotions that can help buffer against stress and challenges. This resilience allows you to navigate difficult situations with greater clarity and adaptability.

Improved relationships: Expressing gratitude towards others strengthens your relationships and deepens your connections. When you show appreciation for the people in your life, it fosters a sense of belonging and strengthens social bonds. This positive social support contributes to your overall well-being and mental clarity.

Heightened creativity: Gratitude opens your mind to new possibilities and enhances your creativity. By focusing on the abundance in your life, you cultivate a mindset of abundance, which allows you to think more creatively and explore innovative solutions to problems. This expanded perspective and creative thinking contribute to mental clarity and fresh insights.

Increased positivity and happiness: Gratitude has a direct impact on your overall happiness and well-being. When you regularly practice gratitude, it creates a positive feedback loop, where you notice and appreciate more positive experiences. This positivity spills over into other areas of your life, boosting your mood, increasing your overall happiness, and providing mental clarity.

In conclusion, cultivating gratitude in your daily life is a powerful tool for enhancing mental clarity. By intentionally focusing on the things you are grateful for, you shift your perspective, reduce stress, and improve your overall well-being. Through gratitude, you gain a greater sense of self-awareness, resilience, and creativity. So, embrace the practice of gratitude and experience the transformative effects it has on your mental clarity and quality of life.

Chapter 40: Embracing the journey to lasting freedom from overthinking.

———

C ongratulations! You have reached the final chapter of this book, and by now, you have gained valuable insights and strategies to overcome overthinking and cultivate mental clarity. However, it's essential to remember that this journey is not a one-time fix but a lifelong process of growth and self-discovery. In this chapter, we will explore the importance of embracing the ongoing journey towards lasting freedom from overthinking.

Embracing self-compassion: As you continue on your path to freedom from overthinking, it's crucial to practice self-compassion. Understand that setbacks and challenges are a normal part of the process. Be kind to yourself when you encounter difficulties, and remember that each step forward is a step closer to lasting change.

Maintaining mindfulness: Mindfulness is a powerful tool that can support you throughout your journey. Continue to cultivate mindfulness practices such as meditation, deep breathing, and present-moment awareness. These practices will help you stay grounded, centered, and connected to the present moment, reducing the likelihood of falling back into old patterns of overthinking.

Embracing growth and learning: View your journey to lasting freedom from overthinking as an opportunity for growth and personal development. Embrace the lessons learned from each experience, whether they are successes or challenges. Every step you take, every decision you make, contributes to your growth and helps you become more resilient and self-aware.

Cultivating resilience: Recognize that setbacks and obstacles are natural parts of life. Building resilience will help you bounce back from setbacks and continue on your journey towards freedom from overthinking. Cultivate a mindset that embraces challenges as opportunities for growth and see each setback as a chance to learn and improve.

Seeking support: Remember that you don't have to embark on this journey alone. Seek support from loved ones, friends, or professionals who can provide guidance, encouragement, and accountability. Surround yourself with a supportive community that understands and supports your desire for lasting freedom from overthinking.

Celebrating progress: Acknowledge and celebrate your progress along the way. Celebrate small victories and milestones, as they are indicators of your growth and dedication. Recognize the positive changes you have made in your thinking patterns, behavior, and overall well-being. Celebrating your progress reinforces your motivation and commitment to the journey.

Embracing flexibility and adaptability: Understand that life is ever-changing, and so are your needs and circumstances. Embrace flexibility and adaptability as you continue your journey. Be open to adjusting your strategies, exploring new techniques, and modifying your approach based on what works best for you in different situations.

Cultivating gratitude: Maintain a practice of gratitude as you progress on your journey. Gratitude keeps you grounded, helps you appreciate the present moment, and reminds you of the progress you have made. By cultivating gratitude, you continue to cultivate a positive mindset and enhance your overall well-being.

Enjoying the process: Remember that the journey itself is valuable. Embrace the process of self-discovery, self-improvement, and personal growth. Enjoy the moments of insight, the small wins, and the transformation that occurs along the way. Find joy in the present moment and savor the progress you make, no matter how small it may seem.

Embracing lifelong learning: Recognize that the journey towards lasting freedom from overthinking is a continuous process of learning and self-improvement. Commit to a lifelong pursuit of knowledge, growth, and self-awareness. Stay curious, explore new perspectives, and be open to ongoing personal and professional development.

In conclusion, embracing the journey to lasting freedom from overthinking is a transformative and rewarding experience. By practicing self-compassion, maintaining mindfulness, embracing growth and learning, cultivating resilience, seeking support, celebrating progress, embracing flexibility and adaptability, cultivating gratitude, enjoying the process, and embracing lifelong learning, you will continue to move forward on your path.

Remember that the journey may have its ups and downs, but each step you take is a step towards breaking free from the chains of overthinking. Be patient with yourself and trust in your ability to navigate through the challenges that may arise.

As you progress, you will notice a positive shift in your mental clarity, overall well-being, and the way you approach life. You will gain a deeper understanding of yourself, your thoughts, and your emotions, allowing you to respond to situations with greater wisdom and clarity.

During this journey, it is important to stay committed to your personal growth and prioritize your well-being. This may involve setting boundaries, saying no to excessive commitments, and taking time for self-care. Remember that taking care of yourself is not selfish but essential for your overall well-being and the sustainability of your progress.

Along the way, you may encounter setbacks or moments of doubt. It is crucial to stay resilient and maintain a positive mindset. Remind yourself of the progress you have already made and the strength within you to overcome any obstacles that may come your way.

Celebrate every milestone and achievement, no matter how small. By acknowledging your progress and accomplishments, you reinforce your motivation and inspire yourself to keep going. Surround yourself with a supportive network of friends, family, or like-minded individuals who can uplift you and provide encouragement throughout your journey.

As you continue to embrace the journey, you will develop a deep sense of self-awareness and an appreciation for the present moment. You will become more attuned to your thoughts and emotions, allowing you to respond intentionally rather than reactively. This newfound clarity will not only benefit you but also your relationships, work, and overall quality of life.

Remember, the journey to lasting freedom from overthinking is a personal one, unique to each individual. Embrace your own path, honor your progress, and be kind to yourself throughout the process. Trust in yourself and your ability to create the life you desire—one that is free from the constraints of overthinking.

In conclusion, by embracing the ongoing journey towards lasting freedom from overthinking, you are committing to a life of self-awareness, growth, and mental clarity. This journey is a continuous process that requires patience, resilience, and self-compassion. Stay committed, seek support when needed, celebrate your progress, and embrace the lifelong adventure of self-discovery. As you do, you will experience the transformational power of breaking free from overthinking and living a life of greater clarity, peace, and fulfillment.

CONGRATULATIONS ON completing "Break free from overthinking: 40 Strategies for stress relief and mental clarity." You have taken a significant step towards liberating yourself from the burden of overthinking and embracing a life of clarity, peace, and fulfillment. Throughout this book, you have explored various techniques, practices, and mindset shifts that empower you to overcome overthinking and live with greater presence and purpose.

Remember that breaking free from overthinking is not a one-time achievement but an ongoing journey. It requires consistent effort, self-awareness, and a commitment to practicing the strategies you have learned. Embrace the power of self-reflection and continue to refine your understanding of your own patterns of overthinking.

As you navigate the challenges and uncertainties that life presents, remember the tools you have gained: mindfulness, gratitude, self-care, setting boundaries, and more. These are your allies in maintaining mental clarity and finding inner peace. When you find yourself slipping into old habits of overthinking, return to the strategies that resonate with you the most and bring yourself back to the present moment.

Share your newfound wisdom with others, for we all experience moments of overthinking. Support and uplift those around you, offering guidance and understanding. Together, we can create a community that thrives on clarity, compassion, and growth.

Always remember that you have the power to break free from the overthinking trap. Trust in your ability to make conscious choices, let go of what no longer serves you, and embrace the beauty of the present moment. Embrace imperfections, practice self-compassion, and honor your unique journey.

As you close this book, carry with you the lessons, insights, and practices that resonate with you the most. Let them serve as a reminder that you possess the strength, resilience, and wisdom to navigate any challenges that come your way. Trust in the process, trust in yourself.

May your life be filled with clarity, peace, and a deep sense of fulfillment. Embrace the journey of breaking free from overthinking, and may it lead you to a life of joy, purpose, and abundant possibilities. Remember, you are the master of your thoughts, and the power to create the life you desire lies within you.

Wishing you all the best on your path to lasting freedom from overthinking.

With gratitude and encouragement, Benjamin Drath

Milton Keynes UK
Ingram Content Group UK Ltd.
UKHW021328280723
425958UK00015B/500